WALKING GRAN PARADISO NATIONAL PARK

30 DAY WALKS IN THE AOSTA VALLEY AND PIEDMONT

by Gillian Price

CICERONE

JUNIPER HOUSE, MURLEY MOSS,
OXENHOLME ROAD, KENDAL, CUMBRIA LA9 7RL
www.cicerone.co.uk

Fourth edition 2025
ISBN: 978 1 78631 183 2
eISBN: 978 1 78765 194 4
Third edition 2018, Second edition 2008, First edition 1997

Printed in Singapore by KHL Printing on responsibly sourced paper.
Cicerone's EU representative for GPSR compliance is Easy Access System Europe, Mustamäe tee 50, 10621 Tallinn, Estonia. Email gpsr.requests@easproject.com.
A catalogue record for this book is available from the British Library.
All photographs are by Gillian Price and Nicola Regine unless otherwise stated.

lovelljohns.com
Route mapping by Lovell Johns www.lovelljohns.com
Contains OpenStreetMap.org data © OpenStreetMap contributors, CC-BY-SA. NASA relief data courtesy of ESRI

Updates to this guide

While every effort is made by our authors to ensure the accuracy of guidebooks as they go to print, changes can occur during the lifetime of an edition. Any updates that we know of for this guide will be on the Cicerone website (www.cicerone.co.uk/1183/updates), so please check before planning your trip. We also advise that you check information about such things as transport, accommodation and shops locally. Even rights of way can be altered over time.

The route maps in this guide are derived from publicly available data, databases and crowd-sourced data. As such they have not been through the detailed checking procedures that would generally be applied to a published map from an official mapping agency, although naturally we have reviewed them closely in the light of local knowledge as part of the preparation of this guide.

We are always grateful for information about any discrepancies between a guidebook and the facts on the ground, sent by email to updates@cicerone.co.uk.

Register your book: To sign up to receive free updates, special offers and GPX files where available, create a Cicerone account and register your purchase via the 'My Account' tab at www.cicerone.co.uk.

Front cover: The Gran Paradiso peak can be admired near Gran Collet (Walk 13)

CONTENTS

Dedication

To Nicola with all my love. Grazie mille for your wonderful company

Acknowledgements

My keen walking companions from visits past and recent were Hatsumi, Piero, Bruno, Grazia, Edda and Giampietro, and the Story family.

Special thanks to Wouter and Pieter for Punta Pousset updated track notes and photos, then Davide of Rifugio Pontese as well as Andy and Lucie for extra photos.

I would like to acknowledge the golden eagles and lammergeiers, along with the majestic ibex, shy chamois and comical marmots – too numerous to name individually – who make this area so special.

Mountain safety

Every mountain walk has its dangers, and those described in this guidebook are no exception. All who walk or climb in the mountains should recognise this and take responsibility for themselves and their companions along the way. The author and publisher have made every effort to ensure that the information contained in this guide was correct when it went to press, but, except for any liability that cannot be excluded by law, they cannot accept responsibility for any loss, injury or inconvenience sustained by any person using this book.

International distress signal *(emergency only)*
Six blasts on a whistle (and flashes with a torch after dark) spaced evenly for one minute, followed by a minute's pause. Repeat until an answer is received. The response is three signals per minute followed by a minute's pause.

Helicopter rescue
The following signals are used to communicate with a helicopter:

Help needed: raise both arms above head to form a 'Y'

Help not needed: raise one arm above head, extend other arm downward

Emergency telephone numbers
General emergency tel 112
Soccorso alpino (mountain rescue) tel 118

Weather reports
https://cf.regione.vda.it/

Mountain rescue can be very expensive – be adequately insured.

After Maison comes a lovely scenic stretch looking to Cima di Courmaon (Walk 25)

Symbols used on route maps

- route
- alternative route
- start point
- finish point
- start/finish point
- alternative finish point
- route direction
- glacier
- woodland
- urban areas
- international border
- station/railway
- bus stop/station
- cable car
- chair lift
- parking
- peak
- manned/unmanned refuge
- building
- cross
- pass
- water feature
- bridge
- other feature
- accommodation
- refreshment
- tourist information

Relief
in metres

4000–4200
3800–4000
3600–3800
3400–3600
3200–3400
3000–3200
2800–3000
2600–2800
2400–2600
2200–2400
2000–2200
1800–2000
1600–1800
1400–1600
1200–1400
1000–1200
800–1000
600–800

SCALE: 1:25,000

0 kilometres 0.25 0.5
0 miles 0.25

SCALE: 1:50,000

0 kilometres 0.5 1
0 miles 0.5

Contour lines are drawn at 25m intervals and highlighted at 100m intervals.

GPX files for all routes can be downloaded free at www.cicerone.co.uk/1183/GPX.

ROUTE SUMMARY TABLE

Walk	Title	Distance	Ascent/ Descent	Grade	Time	Page
1	The Lillaz Waterfalls	2.5km	130m	1–2	1hr 30min	36
2	Lago di Loie	12km	825m	2	5hr	38
3	Vallon de Valeille	9km	300m	1–2	2hr 50min	41
4	Cascades de Pila	6.5km	280m	1–2	2hr 20min	44
5	Laghi di Lussert	19km	1200m	2	6hr 20min	47
6	Montseuc	3.6km	330m	2	2hr	51
7	The Money Glacier Terrace	15.7km	815m	2	6hr	53
8	The Casolari dell'Herbetet Traverse	19.4km	1100m	2–3	7hr 20min	57
9	Punta Pousset	13.7km	1570m	3	7hr 30min	61
10	Beneath the Grivola	12.5km	1440m/ 1710m	2–3	6hr 30min	64
11	Pont d'Ael's Roman Bridge	6km	160m/ 420m	2	2hr	68
12	At the Foot of the Gran Paradiso	14.5km	1180m/ 1040m	2	6hr	72
13	The Gran Collet Circuit	11km	870m	2	4hr 30min	76
14	The King's Path in Valle delle Meyes	13km	830m	2	5hr	80
15	Orvieille and Lacs de Djouan	15.5km	1025m/ 885m	2	5hr	84
16	The 2205m Mont Blanc	12km	1025m	2	5hr	88

Walk	Title	Distance	Ascent/ Descent	Grade	Time	Page
17	Vallon di Sort and Vallon di Entrelor	9.2km	850m	2	4hr 30min	91
18	Rifugio Benevolo and Lago Goletta	13km	860m	2	5hr	94
19	Lakes above Pian del Nivolet	6.6km	260m	2	2hr 30min	97
20	The Royal track to Ceresole Reale	24km	1080m/ 2100m	2–3	8hr	101
21	Lago Serrù Sentiero Glaciologico	4.6km	160m	1–2	2hr	107
22	Upper Valle Orco	11.2km	785m/ 660m	2	5hr 15min	110
23	Beneath the Tre Levanne	16km	1080m	2–3	6hr 45min	113
24	Ceresole Reale lake circuit	7.6km	130m	1	2hr	117
25	The Old Villages of Valle Orco	6.4km	540m	1–2	3hr 30min	120
26	Rifugio Pontese and Lago di Teleccio	7km	450m	1–2	2hr 45min	123
27	Nivolastro to Andorina	8.5km	670m	2	3hr 30min	127
28	Val di Forzo, Boschettiera and Bivacco Davito	11.6km	1100m	2	6hr	130
29	Sanctuary of San Besso	13.3km	1050m	2	5hr 30min	133
30	Above Piamprato to Col Larissa	12.6km	1050m	2	5hr	137

Looking down over the Lillaz waterfalls (Walk 1)

INTRODUCTION

The Tre Levanne rise beyond Lago Agner and Serru on the Piedmont flanks of the park

THE GRAN PARADISO NATIONAL PARK

Located in northwest Italy, spreading over the Valle d'Aosta and Piemonte (or Piedmont) regions, the historical Gran Paradiso National Park is synonymous with majestic soaring mountains and rugged valleys home to fascinating wildlife.

'Intending visitors to the district should be warned that when the King of Italy is hunting around Cogne (the present King has not been there since 1885) they may find their movements impeded by fear of disturbing the game. This will seem however but a small hindrance when set against the great facilities which the royal hunting paths (passable for horses) afford to travellers on the less interesting portions of many of the ascents in this group.'

This introduction appeared in 1893 in *The Mountains of Cogne* (by George Yeld and Reverend WAB Coolidge), one of the first guides to be published. Hunting was prohibited back in 1821 – except by royal entourages – ostensibly to protect the ibex and chamois populations, which were at worryingly low levels, and in 1856 King Vittorio Emanuele II declared a Royal Game Reserve. Five hunting lodges were constructed along with 350km of tracks, all manned by a veritable army of gamekeepers (mostly converted poachers), beaters and porters.

Then in 1922 his son King Vittorio Emanuele III took a landmark step and gave up his hunting rights, declaring Italy's very first national park 'for the purpose of protecting the fauna and flora, and preserving the special geological formations, as well as the beauty of the scenery'. Nowadays it encompasses 700km^2 with 470km of marked paths linking alpine meadows below magnificent mountains and glaciers, wild valleys and traditional hamlets. A team of 50 rangers monitor wildlife.

WALKS

This guidebook describes 30 selected day routes across the Gran Paradiso Park, ranging from 1hr 30min to a whopping 8 hours. Base yourself at a village hotel, apartment, campsite or rifugio and take walks out in different directions. Altitudes range from 1000 metres above sea level to over 3000 metres. In between are relaxing strolls along rivers, across flowered meadows and through conifer woods, testing steep climbs over rough unstable terrain (inevitably followed by knee-knocking descents) and even cool snowfield traverses.

There is plenty of variety and options for all legs and lungs. Walkers will enjoy unforgettable days on excellent trails through spectacular valleys that they often have all to themselves, even at the height of the summer season. Remember that the further you venture away from 'civilisation' and the valley settlements, the wilder and more exciting the scenery becomes and the fewer two-legged visitors you are likely to meet.

GRAN PARADISO

The romantic name Gran Paradiso goes back much further than the kings. The national park took its name from the 4061m mountain (the only 4000+m summit wholly in Italy), probably derived from *granta parei* 'great wall', if not from the host of saintly peaks at the head of Valnontey – San Pietro, San Andrea and Sant'Orso.

The first recorded ascent was in 1860, by English climbers JJ Cowell and W Dundas with French guides Michel Payot and Jean Tairraz. As they weren't equipped with crampons, they had to cut over 1000 steps in the ice! The ascent did not immediately become popular, so to encourage visitors in 1931, the mountaineer-priest Abbé Henry took a donkey called Cagliostro to the summit, fitting his hoofs with iron nails: 'If donkeys can go up the Gran Paradiso, then so can people...'. Modern-day visitors are advised to engage the services of a qualified alpine guide for the mixed rock and ice route.

What's more, long-distance walkers with an adventurous bent can embark on the superb 12-day Alta Via 2 (see the separate Cicerone guide *Trekking Gran Paradiso: Alta Via 2*).

Should these not suffice, enquire at local tourist offices for further suggestions – there are plenty more!

SOME GEOLOGY

Part of the Graian Alps, the Gran Paradiso group started out over 230 million years ago as volcanic material, with a fraction of marine sediments. Tectonic activity led in fits and starts to the formation of the Alps during the Tertiary period (about 54 to 57 million years ago), the accompanying heat and pressure responsible for the transformation into metamorphic rock. The Gran Paradiso summit, for instance, is made up of a huge dome of augen-gneiss girdled by calcareous rock, mica-schists and greenstone.

Immense mineral deposits have proved to be of great economic significance to humanity since pre-Roman times, first and foremost the magnetite extracted at Cogne up until 1979 and processed at the Aosta steelworks. The original name of the Valle Orco, the southern valley, was 'Eva d'or' (water of gold) because of the precious minerals in its sands.

Walkers heading down the royal track (Walk 20)

The meadows at Cogne in the Aosta valley look up to magnificent glaciated peaks

A total of 57 glaciers of varying dimensions are scattered across the park, but rather than rivers of ice, observant visitors will notice a wide range of related phenomena: vast rock slabs polished smooth by ancient glacier passage, as well as groups of 'roches moutonnées', rounded rocks known for their similarity to recumbent sheep. Then there are U-shaped valleys crafted by long-gone glaciers, without forgetting erratics or huge boulders transported far from their starting place by the ice flow.

HYDROELECTRICITY AND DAMS

Naturally, glaciers provide abundant meltwater so rivers, streams, waterfalls and lakes are plentiful. Back in the 1920s this attracted hydroelectric dam builders keen to respond to the needs of the expanding industry of Torino. They began operations in the Piedmont's Valle Orco, damming lakes at Ceresole Reale, Teleccio, Serrù, Agnel, Valsoera, and Eugio. Remarkable engineering feats, they are connected with giant underground conduits (often twinned with lifts for staff) and continue to supply the historic power plant at Rosone among others.

However, the most obvious are the moraines; chaotic ridges of debris transported by ice flow and deposited at its sides or front, left high and dry after the glacier's retreat. These help understand the history of the area: for example, bare moraine probably dates back to the last mini-ice age, a mere 300 years ago. On average, 5000 years must pass before such a ridge can be colonised by pioneer plants, following preparatory work by lichens. Trees such as larch or dwarf mountain pine need even longer (15,000 years in all) before the soil is suitable for them to take root. Walk 21 follows a *sentiero glaciologico* (glacier-related path) where many of these phenomena can be observed.

SOME HISTORY

The Gran Paradiso National Park straddles two administrative and political regions of Italy – the Valle d'Aosta in the north and Piemonte in the south (Piedmont in English).

Historical highlights include the Roman era, when the city of Augusta Praetoria – present-day Aosta – was founded in 25BC as a strategic alpine junction on the Via delle Gallie. Rather later on, the Aosta valley was controlled by the Savoy dynasty, almost without interruption, from the 11th century up until 1861, when Italy was unified. French was the main language and is still taught and used, along with Italian, these days (the region is officially bilingual). However, in addition, many inhabitants speak Valdôtain, an unusual patois of French-Provençal origin that embraces a wealth of specialised vocabulary for pastoral activities and the natural surrounds, which persist in place names and on maps.

Demographically, the mid-1800s saw a significant growth in population which put a strain on natural resources. This led to seasonal emigration of itinerant tinkers, seed-sellers, chimney sweeps and glaziers from the southern valleys in particular. Later on, large-scale emigration became a permanent fixture, and expat communities such as the one in Paris have actually helped preserve the Valle Soana dialect. Contact with home villages is kept up and French number plates are commonplace in village car parks during the holiday period.

These days around 300 people reportedly call the Gran Paradiso National Park area home, in sharp contrast to 8359 in 1981, and the 1881 peak of 20,616. Villages and hamlets have been progressively abandoned and walkers will find themselves wandering along age-old paths through long-empty houses.

WILDLIFE

One of the main reasons for visiting the Gran Paradiso is the marvellous opportunity for observing wildlife at close quarters. To state the obvious, the best way to spot animals is to look around for them – most are masters of disguise and perfectly camouflaged in their natural habitat. Desolate rock-strewn cirques often reveal fawn patches which, on closer inspection, turn out to be chamois. Grassy ground is pitted with marmot burrows while abandoned farm buildings overgrown with nettles may be home to reptiles. Uninviting rock crests are worth perusing with binoculars for the likelihood of ibex sentinels – often tracking the progress of walkers!

The elegant ibex, *Capra ibex*, is the undisputed king and star of the Gran Paradiso. Also known as bouquetin or steinbock, this stocky wild goat is easily recognisable from a distance for its enormous backward-curving ribbed horns, which grow almost to one metre on males, half for females. Males can weigh up to 90kg, females up to 50kg and both live for around 10 years. Well established and protected, they now number around 3000, in contrast to the 300 reported by Yeld and Coolidge in 1893 and the 400 survivors after World War 2. It was the original Gran Paradiso ibex that repopulated the whole of alpine Europe. So numerous are they that walkers go close to bumping into them at times!

They were considered 'walking pharmacies' as their blood, horns, bones and even droppings were used in remedies for poisoning to rheumatism. They had been hunted intensely since medieval times, and a talisman fashioned from the tiny cross-shaped bone found in its heart was believed to guard the wearer against violent death.

Male ibex grazing

A chamois on the lookout for food

Of a summer's evening, young males clash horns in mock battle in preparation for the December mating season. (Then it is anything but pretend with the females only on heat for 24 hours.) Sedate older males graze unperturbed, some distance from herds of timid females with their young.

Fleet-footed chamois, *Rupicapra rupicapra*, abound – a recent count gave 7700 in the park. Slender and daintier, they sport short hooked horns, pale fawn coats and white patches on face and rear. Their principal predators are foxes and eagles but long snowy winters also take a big toll on both ibex and chamois populations. Curiously, neither animal loses their horns on an annual basis, in contrast to the red and roe deer which inhabit lower wooded slopes.

It is hard to miss hearing the European alpine marmot, *Marmota marmota*, with its shrill whistle warning of imminent danger, or seeing a well-padded rear scampering over grassy hillocks towards its burrow. These comical beaver-like vegetarians live in large underground colonies and 8000–10,000 were reported recently. Protected now, they were once hunted for their fat, used in ointments believed to be a cure for rheumatism. The belief was unfounded, however, and the practice seemingly arose from a linguistic misunderstanding: the real 'marmot oil' for treating aches and pains comes from the so-called marmot plum or Briançon apricot.

Red foxes are often spotted outside a rifugio at nightfall, as they come to scavenge titbits in the rubbish. Much more difficult to spot is the elegant wolf, *Canis lupus*. Originally from the central Italian Apennines, they have stealthily spread across the Alps with two established packs here. The rangers say the park is their personal supermarket and in return they help keep the hoofed animal population in check.

Another sizeable carnivore returning gradually westward across the Alps is the lynx. Sightings of the tufted-ear feline with grey-brown mottled fur have been reported in Valle d'Aosta, where it prefers the shelter of low-altitude woods, the habitat of its favourite prey, the roe deer. It is also known to hunt old ibex who are slower on their feet.

Last but not least is the wild boar. Not a native, it was introduced to populate neighbouring hunting reserves and has bred so successfully that it is becoming a nuisance, wreaking havoc in the chestnut woods. Their numbers are so high in Valle Orco that the park rangers have to spend valuable time capturing them.

As amphibians go, the common frog is renowned for its ability to spend winters frozen into lakes up 2500m, thawing back to life in spring. On dry southern hillsides the bright emerald sheen of the green lizard is hard to miss, while snakes sun themselves on paths and old stone walls. The most common is the poisonous and protected adder alias viper. This greyish-brown snake has a diamond-shaped head and zigzag pattern along its back. Extremely timid, it only attacks when threatened, so do give it time to slither away should you encounter one. In the unlikely circumstance that someone is bitten, keep calm, stay put and seek medical help as soon as possible. Bandaging is usually recommended in the meantime.

Higher up glide ubiquitous flocks of chaotic noisy orange-beaked crows, more correctly known as alpine choughs. Great chatty socialisers, they appear out of nowhere at strategic cols at the rustling of a food wrapper in the sure knowledge that they will be fed by walkers' crumbs. Their only equals in noise are the raucous European jays, which flash

A well-fed marmot

blue feathers on their dashes through the mixed woods lower down. Then there's the voracious nutcracker. Easily spotted perching on treetops, the industrious dappled crow-like bird is an expert at cracking pine cones with its thick beak. It is responsible for the survival of the Arolla pine as it hoards its kernels in rock crannies then forgets where 20% is hidden, so the trees sprout and grow in the most unlikely spots.

Impressive shadows are cast by majestic golden eagles (27 couples call the park home), who have a field day in summer preying on young marmots, not to mention chamois and ibex; amazingly a 7kg eagle can fly off with prey weighing up to 20kg! They have reportedly perfected the hunting technique of knocking wild animals off crests.

Their only competition in terms of territory comes from the largest bird in the Alps, the lammergeier or bearded vulture. Slightly larger than the eagle it boasts a three-metre wing span while its orange neck ruff and wedge-shaped tail distinguish it from the rounded tail of the eagle. Not a hunter, it prefers carcasses. It is able to swallow bones up to 30cm in length (digestion then requiring 24 hours!), and cracks bones by dropping them from a great height to get to the marrow. The reintroduction of lammergeiers born in captivity took off in 1986 in Austria and 1994 saw the first release in Italy. Sightings are not unusual as the park boasts three couples. An impressive stuffed specimen is on display at the Chavaney (Val di Rhêmes) Park Visitor Centre.

Other treats are the brilliant swirling clouds of butterflies which vie with each for brightness – such as the metallic hues of the common blue Icarus butterfly which flutter up from their puddles when disturbed. The rare Red Apollo perches on thistles, pale grey-cream but with trademark black and red 'eyes' on its wings.

Last on the list is the so-called glacier flea, which forms dark patches on the surface of glaciers and snow fields up to 3800m. It is one to two millimetres long, hairy or scaly, mottled brown and feeds on organic matter such as pollen carried up by the wind. Red-tinted snow on the other hand may either mean cold-loving algae with a blood-red colouring or sand from a far-off desert, incredible though it may seem.

PLANTS AND FLOWERS

An excellent place to admire the remarkable array of alpine plants is the attractive 10,000m^2 Giardino Botanico Alpino 'Paradisia' in Valnontey, established in 1955 and named after the St Bruno lily, *Paradisia liliastrum*. Over the summer, 1000 labelled alpine species flourish there – a good 250 are found wild in the park.

The woods are mainly mixed conifer, dominated by larch and Arolla pine, along with juniper

Clockwise from top left: Orchids are at home in meadows; Glacier crowfoot can grow at incredible altitudes; Unusual purple asters; Gentians come in a variety of shapes and shades; Leopard's-bane is a favourite with chamois

shrubs. Curious diminutive versions of trees such as the net-leaved willow and ice-age relict dwarf birch are common. This habitat is shared with pretty pink alpenrose shrubs, wine-red martagon lilies and bilberry and cowberry plants with their minute creamy flowers which pave the way for late-summer fruit.

As flowers go, the record-holder for altitude is the glacier crowfoot, which grows up to 4200m. Also high up are colonisers of screes and bare rock, such as lilac round-leaved pennycress and succulent saxifrage ('rock breaker') which penetrate cracks. Further down, stunning carpets of white ranunculus and pasque flowers smother pasture basins such as the Piano del Nivolet. Marshland is often punctuated with soft white cotton grass and tiny carnivorous butterworts, both blue-violet or the yellow-white alpine variety. The famous edelweiss is relatively unusual due to a lack of the calcareous terrain it prefers. The delicate pink-white drooping twinflower, which grows on moss cushions on open grassland, is a rare treat not to mention an ice-age relict. Elegant lilac orchids are widespread in meadows; the dark reddish-brown black vanilla variety has a surprisingly strong cocoa aroma. Curious purple asters share the terrain. Gentians also love meadows and come in a surprising range of shapes and colours – from the piercing blue of the trumpet variety through to the purplish willow gentian and the pale yellow and spotted types.

The alpine environment is extremely hostile to life in general and the growth and reproduction season for high-altitude vegetation can be as short as 60–70 days. Each species has developed survival techniques, ranging from thick hairy layers as protection from cold winds and evaporation (edelweiss), antifreeze in its leaves (glacier crowfoot), as well as ground-hugging forms that minimise exposure, allow the plant to exploit the heat from the earth and ensure protective snow cover (cushions of rock jasmine). In addition to the beating they get from the elements, many also risk being nibbled by chamois (who have a weakness for sugary large-flowered leopard's-bane) and marmots (who go for forget-me-nots) and even being picked by humans.

To end on a 'spiritual' note, a quick mention is in order for the insignificant-looking but strongly aromatic yellow genipi, found on stony grassland. Although it is both rare and protected, local residents are allowed to gather a limited number to prepare their beloved Genepì spirit – a perfect after-dinner drink with guaranteed digestive properties to boot.

A recommended rucksack companion for flower lovers is the Cicerone pocket guide *Alpine Flowers* (2019), while Grey-Wilson and Blamey's *Alpine Flowers of Britain and Europe* (Harper Collins, 1995) is the perfect reference book at home.

The old track boasts vast views (Walk 22)

HOW TO GET THERE

By air

The most convenient airport is Torino's Caselle www.aeroportoditorino.it/en, well served from the UK and European countries. Private transfers go direct to Aosta (www.transfervallee.eu/en), otherwise regular local trains and buses convey passengers to the city centre and the main railway station, Torino Porta Nuova, for ongoing services.

Milano is also handy and has two airports, both well served by UK, European and international companies. Both Malpensa www.milanomalpensa-airport.com and Linate www.milanolinate-airport.com have direct trains to Milano Centrale station for links via Chivasso to the Valle d'Aosta or via Torino Porta Susa for the railway line to Pont Canavese – see below.

By car

Drivers have a good choice of itineraries, which are pretty spectacular: from France via the Mont Blanc tunnel or the Piccolo San Bernardo pass; from Switzerland via the Gran San Bernardo pass and tunnel. From the south, as well as main SS26, the A5 autostrada (motorway) leads via Aosta to Courmayeur. For the southern section you'll need SS460 from Torino via Cuorgné and on to Pont Canavese.

By coach and train

From the north, Valle d'Aosta can be approached by coach from France via Chamonix or from Switzerland via Martigny. Otherwise, you can arrive from the south by train via Ivrea as far as Aosta. Long-distance coaches also run from Torino and Milano.

The southern flanks of the Park are accessible from Torino, which in turn has international rail connections via Modane in France. From Torino take the train as far as Pont Canavese.

LOCAL TRANSPORT

Train information is available at www.trenitalia.com, tel 892021. Remember to stamp train tickets in one of the machines at the platform before you travel; failure to do so can result in a fine. The exception are tickets with a booked seat (showing date and time).

For bus info ask at local tourist offices. In Aosta, you can get information at the central bus station (*autostazione*) (tel 0165 262027) across the road from the railway station.

When reading timetables or asking for information, remember that *giornaliero* (abbreviated as GG) means daily, *scolastico* means during school term, *feriale* means Monday to Saturday, and *festivo* means Sunday or public holidays. *Sciopero* means strike.

Services are reliable and reasonably priced. Summer timetables take effect around mid-June, ending in September, depending on school term dates.

Bus companies and destinations

Arriva
https://aosta.arriva.it
Serves the main valley including Aosta, as well as Val di Rhêmes and Valsavarenche. They also have a direct Milano–Aosta bus and a Torino–Aosta run as well as to Torino's Casselle airport.

Ceresole Reale Tourist Office
Tel 0124 953186
www.turismoceresolereale.it
For the free summer shuttle buses from Locana via Ceresole Reale to Colle del Nivolet.

Cogne Tourist Office
www.cogneturismo.it Tel 0165 74040
For the free Cogne shuttle bus (to Valnontey, Lillaz and Gimillan).

FLIXBUS
www.flixbus.it
Runs to Aosta from Milano and Torino and several airports.

GTT
Tel 800 019152 (tel 011 0672000 from a mobile) www.gtt.to.it
Does runs via Rivarolo and Pont Canavese railway stations to Ceresole Reale, as well as a service via Ronco Canavese to Piamprato.

SVAP
www.svap.it
Runs up the Cogne valley.

Trekbus

Bookings at tel 380 9010162 info@cm-grandparadis.vda.it

An on-demand minibus links the Gran Paradiso valleys (Cogne, Valsavarenche, Val di Rhêmes, Valgrisenche) July–mid-September if there is no public bus handy.

WHEN TO GO

The park area is open year-long. The most suitable period for walkers is June to October. Then the winter snow has usually melted and the high-altitude rifugi are open. Early summer walkers planning on high-altitude walks should take micro spikes in case of icy conditions. During the winter months most routes will be under metres of snow and ice.

July is probably the best month for flower lovers, while August is the busiest as it's peak holiday time in Europe. Late summer–autumn brings crystal-clear days, stunning autumn colours and very few people on the paths. Italy stays on summer time until the end of October, meaning a bonus of extra daylight for visitors. The choice is yours.

VALLEYS AND BASES

The steep-sided valleys that push their way towards the heart of the Gran Paradiso Park from all sides spell convenient access for visitors. All are inhabited and have plenty of facilities with beds for all pockets (hotels, B&Bs, camping grounds and high-altitude rifugi – see Accommodation). What's more, they can be reached by public bus and train (see Local transport).

Starting on the Park's northern edge and the Aosta valley, key Vallon di Cogne forks S-SE near Aymavilles. One of the Park's outstanding destinations, it has a wealth of well-kept farming settlements amidst dazzling landscapes and walking routes (Walks 1–11). A glorious pasture flat is home to former mining centre Cogne, now a bustling well-served visitor hub with sleeping options, eateries and shops. Minor valleys fork off here, home to the lovely sister villages of Lillaz, Valnontey and Gimillan, all excellent bases. Tiny Valnontey is arguably the best-placed, not far from the foot of the Tribolazione glacier and its crown of beautiful peaks.

Further west, Valsavarenche (Walks 12–15) slices its way southwards via Dégioz and Eaux Rousses, fine places to stay. The valley opens out and the road goes as far as low-key Pont, gateway to the Gran Paradiso mountain itself. With a decent choice of hotels and camping grounds, this is the place to come.

Forking off from Valsavarenche at Introd is quieter Val di Rhêmes, the westernmost confine of the national park. Here the main settlement is Rhêmes-Notre-Dame which offers a full range of tourist facilities. Further up the valley a scattering of hamlets is dominated by the magnificent Granta

Parei outcrop. Walks 16–18 can be followed from this valley.

The southernmost Piedmont side of the Gran Paradiso has decent access from Torino thanks to the railway line via Rivarolo Canavese as far as Pont (currently undergoing reconstruction), and ongoing bus links. At Pont the valley forks and narrow Valle Soana breaks off north. The village of Ronco Canavese is a suitable base for forays into the surrounding mountains – Walks 27–29. Further up, quiet Piamprato (Walk 30) is another lovely spot.

From Pont the Valle Orco winds its tortuous way west, with a fork at Rosone for Vallone di Piantonetto (Walk 26). Further along is the picturesque if diminutive village of Noasca (Walk 25). Next comes strategic Ceresole Reale set on a lakeside and dam, a well-served base for Walks 22–24. The rambling Grand Hotel dates back to 1888 and provided comfort during sojourns of the Piedmont aristocracy along with lyrical 19th-century Italian poet Carducci. Nowadays it houses a Park Visitor Centre focusing on the ibex.

At the dizzy conclusion of the hairpin bends from Ceresole Reale via a string of dams (and Walk 21) to the head of Valle Orco, is Colle del Nivolet, with a handy rifugio and terminus for summer shuttle buses; Walks 19 and 20 start here.

ACCOMMODATION

The villages of the Gran Paradiso have a good range of hotels, apartments, guesthouses to B&Bs and campsites. Consult local tourist offices (see Appendix B) or online agencies such as booking.com. It's advisable to book in advance in midsummer.

Many of the walks in this book visit a rifugio, a mountain hut that provides shelter, hot meals, refreshments and accommodation during the alpine summer (June to Sept/Oct). An overnight stay in one of these marvellous, scenically placed huts is a memorable experience and can be the highlight of a walking holiday – it's worth trying to factor one in during your trip. They are run by the Italian Alpine Club CAI, as well as local families and alpine guides, and everyone is welcome. They offer reasonably priced meals and drinks and hostel-like dormitories – you need your own sleeping sheet (blankets are plentiful). Bathrooms are shared – take a towel. Toilet paper is provided. Charges start at €15 for a *pernottamento* or overnight stay to €55 for *mezza pensione* or half board (dinner, overnight, breakfast). Contact details for the rifugi visited in this guidebook are in Appendix C.

Additionally there is the *bivacco*, bivouac hut, often a metal container with basic bunk beds or at best, a converted shepherd's hut with running water and wood stove. Located in out-of-the-way spots, they are usually left

At Rifugio Marmotte (Walk 17) (photo by Andrew and Lucie Price)

open for self-sufficient walkers and climbers.

You will also come across mountainside buildings labelled 'Casotto PNGP'. They belong to the park and are for the exclusive use of rangers; they are not for walkers.

Wild camping is strictly forbidden within the bounds of the Gran Paradiso National Park. Please respect this. There are good facilities in the valleys and many camping grounds also have bungalows.

FOOD AND DRINK

Foodies will be delighted with the regional culinary specialities. Look out for polenta concia, a delicious and filling thick cornmeal porridge enriched with local cheese; delicate carbonada, meat stewed in red wine with juniper berries; risotto alla valdostana, a rice dish with melted cheeses such as fontina and toma. Seupetta di Cogne is a thick soup of rice blended with cheese, melted butter, and topped with croutons and cinammon. Zuppa Valpellinentze on the other hand consists of cabbage, brown bread, broth and fontina cheese. Tartiflette is a hearty fry-up of potatoes, onion, lard or pancetta and cheese irrigated with wine. If in doubt when ordering your meal, simply ask *'Qual'è la vostra specialità?'*

As may be obvious, the cheeses of the Valle d'Aosta and Piemonte would

ALPINE CLUBS

Membership of CAI (Club Alpino Italiano) is open to all nationalities. Intending members should apply to individual branches: the complete list can be found at www.cai.it. The annual fee is around €50 with half-price rates for family members and 18–25-year-olds, and less for children. As well as reductions in huts across the Alps, this covers alpine rescue.

Members of many European alpine clubs enjoy reciprocal rights in Italy. Brits can join the UK branch of the Austrian club www.alpenverein.at/britannia.

rate a chapter all their own. Myriad and memorable, they are crafted in small dairy farms which means no two have the same flavour. Using goat, cow and sheep's milk, they range from fresh, delicate and creamy through to mature, strong tasting and strikingly pungent, sometimes left to ripen in cave-cellars for months. Toma refers to a smallish round of cheese, cow more often than not. Fontina, the classic cheese for melting, comes in huge rounds weighing up to 20kg.

Polenta with stewed beef

The southern Canavese valleys produce Brüs, a highly peppered cottage cheese. Lastly sargnun, a tasty ricotta look-alike comes fresh, salted or smoked, consumed with rye-bread known as pane di segale or pane nero. It only used to be baked twice a year so was often eaten rock hard, leading to the invention of wooden bread boards with a built-in chopper; these days thankfully it is served fresh and soft. It is also a perfect match for cured meats and lard, which is sliced tracing-paper thin.

Piemonte style antipasti (starters) feature home-pickled vegetables, sliced prosciutto (ham) and infinite varieties of salami made from *cinghiale* (wild boar), *suino* (pork) and even *asinello* (donkey). A leaner more delicate cured sausage is mocetta: originally made with ibex meat, these days it contains beef marinated in brandy, honey and spices.

One unmissable dessert is crema di Cogne, light chocolate cream thickened with egg and served with crunchy crisp tegole biscuits baked with ground hazelnut and almonds. Needs to be tasted to be believed.

An excellent array of delicious wines comes from the terraced vineyards lining the Valle d'Aosta – see www.lovevda.it/en/food-and-wine/wines. Piemonte wines on the other hand include renowned reds the ilk of Barbera and Nebbiolo. You'll be spoilt for choice. Stronger stuff comes as the aromatic liquor Genepì, known for its digestive properties and made from the flowers of the same name (not to be confused with juniper). Finally, mention must be made of the grolla, a decorated lidded wooden bowl with multiple mouthpieces. It may appear after dinner – filled with a delicious blend of coffee, red wine, grappa, sugar and lemon. This 'cup of friendship' is passed around for measured sips.

WHAT TO TAKE

Essentials start with good quality waterproof boots with ankle support and non-slip soles – preferably not brand new, unless you plan on using lots of bandaids! While normal trainers are totally inadequate for alpine paths, trail running shoes are a good lightweight option – if you're used to them.

Beautiful Plan Borgnoz and its glacial streams (Walk 14)

Taking it easy at Lago di Lauson (Walk 8)

Second on the list is a comfortable lightweight rucksack with waist straps. It needs to be big enough to contain food and drink for a day, along with extra clothing, rain gear (poncho or jacket, over-trousers and rucksack cover) and emergency items including a basic first aid kit. Shoulder bags are totally unsuitable and can be dangerous.

A wide-brimmed hat, sunglasses and high factor protective sun cream are essential – remember that for every 1000m of ascent, the intensity of UV rays increases by 10%. This, combined with lower levels of humidity and pollution which act as filters in other areas, and possible snow cover reflecting UV rays, means that you need a cream with a much higher protection factor than at sea level.

Layers of clothing are needed to cater for fiery sun through to wind, lashing rain, storms and even snow: T-shirts and shorts, comfortable long trousers (not jeans), fleece, windproof jacket and woolly hat and gloves.

Lightweight telescopic trekking poles come in handy on steep slopes, especially for wonky knees.

Don't forget a water bottle and filter.

Although food is available at rifugi on many of the walks described here, it is best to be self-sufficient and carry your own lunch and high-energy snacks. Moreover, bad weather, minor accidents and all manner of unforeseen factors could hold you up on the track, and that extra biscuit or fruit bar could be crucial.

Mineral salt tablets are helpful in combating salt depletion and dehydration caused by profuse sweating; prolonged fatigue and heat stroke symptoms may indicate a problem.

Lacs Trebecchi look towards the Gran Paradiso (Walk 19)

Get hold of a walking map to supplement the maps provided in this book.

Lastly, it's a good idea to carry a whistle, headlamp or torch for calling for help – you can't always rely on your mobile phone – see Emergencies.

MAPS AND GPX TRACKS

The maps in this guidebook give an idea of the routes described with significant landmarks and help with orientation and pre-trip preparation. They are not intended as substitutes for commercial maps. The whole of the Parco Nazionale del Gran Paradiso is covered by a handy double 1:25,000 walking map from L'Escursionista (www.escursionista.it). Fraternali (www.fraternalieditore.com) also does an excellent large format 1:25,000 map.

Both are on sale at bookshops and newspaper kiosks throughout the Gran Paradiso National Park, as well as overseas map outlets and outdoor gear shops.

Appendix A is an Italian–English glossary with a wealth of commonly used terminology.

Note: Due to the region's history, the spelling of place names varies considerably on both signposts and maps and discrepancies are common; for instance, a col may be referred to as either *finestra* in the Italian version or *fenêtre* in French. Moreover, moves are underway re-introducing toponyms in the ancient patois. Be prepared to exercise a little linguistic elasticity when map- and sign-reading.

All the walks described in this guidebook come complete with gpx tracks which can be downloaded from www.cicerone.co.uk/1183/GPX.

DOS AND DON'TS

- Find time to get fit prior to setting out on holiday, as this will make your walks more enjoyable, not to mention safer.

- Read the walk description carefully and begin gradually, choosing walks suited to your experience and fitness.
- Start out as early as possible and always have extra time up your sleeve to allow for detours due to collapsed bridges, wrong turns and missing signposts.
- Check weather forecasts – ask at tourist offices or rifugi. Never set out on a long route if the weather is uncertain. Areas such as ice and snow fields can be submerged in thick layers of mist, making orientation problematic. Rain, wind and snow are tiring and can make even easy paths dangerous. Keep away from crests and metal fixtures during an electrical storm and don't shelter under trees or rock overhangs.
- Tempting though it may often be, especially in descent, don't stray from the path, especially not to cut corners. This causes irreparable erosion and damages vegetation. Remember that your behaviour will encourage others to do the same.
- Carry all your rubbish back down to the valley where it can be disposed of correctly. Even organic waste such as apple cores is best not left lying around as it could upset the diet of animals and birds.
- Be considerate when making a toilet stop. Keep away from streams, don't leave unsightly paper lying around (please carry it away in a plastic bag rather than burying it) and remember that abandoned huts and rock overhangs could serve as life-saving shelter for someone else!
- Wildlife should never be disturbed or handled. Collecting flowers, insects or minerals is strictly forbidden, as are fires and wild camping.
- Always carry extra protective clothing as well as energy foods for emergency situations. Remember that in normal circumstances the temperature drops an average of 6°C for every 1000 metres you climb.
- Learn the international call for help – see Emergencies. Don't rely on your mobile phone as there may not be any signal in remote valleys.
- Check out the advice from the CAI experts at www.montagnamicaesicura.it/inglese/index.html
- Don't take your dog into the Gran Paradiso National Park unless you've checked beforehand as most areas are off limits to them www.pngp.it/en/visit-park/walking-dogs-park.
- Download the PeakFinder app – it's invaluable for identifying all those marvellous mountains you'll see.

EMERGENCIES

All walkers need health insurance cover. Those from the EU need a European Health Insurance Card (EHIC), while UK residents require a UK Global Insurance Card (GHIC – see www.dh.gov.uk.). Holders of both are entitled to free or subsidised emergency treatment in Italy, which has an excellent public health system. Australia has a reciprocal agreement with Italy – see www.medicareaustralia.gov.au. All other nationalities need to take out suitable cover.

In addition, travel insurance to cover an alpine walking holiday is strongly recommended. Membership of alpine clubs includes rescue insurance – see Accommodation.

'Help' is *aiuto* in Italian and 'I need help' is *ho bisogno di aiuto* (o bee-zon-yoh dee eye-yoo-toh). Rifugi staff can always be relied on in emergencies.

Check out the handy GeoResq app from the Italian alpine rescue service www.cnsas.it/en/georesq/.

The international rescue signals may come in handy: the call for help is six signals per minute. These can be visual (such as waving a handkerchief or flashing a torch) or audible (whistling or shouting). They are to be repeated after a one-minute pause. The answer is three visual or audible signals per minute, to be repeated after a one-minute pause. Anyone who sees or hears such a call for help must contact the nearest rifugio or police station as quickly as possible.

The general emergency telephone number in Italy is 112, while calls for *soccorso alpino* (mountain rescue) are best made to 118.

USING THIS GUIDE

The walk descriptions are preceded with a box giving start/finish, walking time, distance, ascent/descent, grade, and access details. The majority of walks in this guide are easily accessible by bus.

Walking time is approximate – everyone walks at a different pace. It does not include pauses for a rest, toilet stop, meals or photos so always add on a couple of hours to be realistic. Groups should remember that their pace will be dictated by their slowest member.

Distance (in kilometres) is nowhere near as important as total ascent/descent aka total height gain and loss (given in metres).

Grade gives an indication of the difficulty of the route. Do remember that adverse weather conditions or snow cover will increase difficulty.

Grade 1 means a straightforward path with moderate slope, suitable for all walkers (*T turistico* on the Italian scale).

Grade 2 means a fairly strenuous alpine walk, but not especially difficult (*E escursionistico* on the Italian scale).

Grade 3 means some experience on alpine terrain is a prerequisite as there may be particularly steep and exposed sections. A head for heights and orientation skills may also come in useful (*EE escursionistico esperto* on the Italian scale).

PATH MARKING

All the paths followed in this guide have numbers and identifying markings, be that paint stripes on tree trunks and prominent stones and/or signposts at junctions. The style varies from red and white paint stripes with a black number in the park's southern Piedmont region (in conformity with the Italian Alpine Club system used nationwide) to a system of yellow and black arrows and stripes in the north, namely the Valle d'Aosta region.

Then there are the lifesaving cairns, appropriately referred to in Italian as *ometti* or little men. These mounds of stones heaped up by thoughtful walkers seem banal but on an uncertain path in low cloud they

Waymarks in Piedmont

Waymarks in the Valle Aosta

stand out like beacons, while painted marks can be swallowed up by the mist.

LOCAL TRADITIONS

A kaleidoscope of cultural events is on offer. In addition to the numerous castles in the Valle d'Aosta, a great attraction are the unusual *'Battailles des Reines'*. Probably traceable back to prehistoric times, they involve two enormous pregnant cows engaged in (bloodless) battle, for the honour of being decorated 'Queen'. Each competitor has already established herself as best milker-cum-battler at the head of a herd. Emotional local tournaments involving entire villages start in March and the grand finale is the Regional Championship held late October in Aosta. The *'calendrier des combats'* is available from tourist offices. The practice is also extended to goats with the *'Bataille des Tzevres'* held in Valgrisenche in September.

Gimillan where Walks 4 and 5 start

Otherwise, long processions to high-altitude sanctuaries are a favourite midsummer activity. Popular local events with a legendary or religious origin, they attract huge crowds, often emigrants who return every year for the occasion. Worthy of mention are the Notre Dame des Neiges procession to Lago Miserin (5 August) and the mammoth San Besso celebrations at Campiglia Soana (10 August), referred to in the relevant walk descriptions.

FURTHER SUGGESTIONS

Walkers ready to embark on a memorable long-distance trek through the Gran Paradiso will enjoy the Alta Via 2 – see the new Cicerone guidebook *Trekking Gran Paradiso: Alta Via 2. From Chardonney to Courmayeur in the Aosta Valley* by Gillian Price.

WALKS

The old game track in Valle de Meyes (Walk 14)

WALK 1

The Lillaz Waterfalls

Start/Finish	Lillaz bus stop and car park
Time	1hr 30min
Distance	2.5km
Ascent/Descent	130m
Grade	1–2
Access	Summer bus from Cogne

In the early summer months as rising temperatures melt the snow, torrents of foaming water come crashing down polished rock chutes into crystal-clear pools above the village of Lillaz. Even at other times of the year the *cascate* (waterfalls) are quite a sight as the modest glaciers upstream ensure a constant supply of water.

Set at the southern end of the popular Vallon di Cogne, this is a straightforward circular walk that includes a number of steep uphill stretches, several with helpful rungs and handrails. Wind-borne spray can make the ground slippery, so youngsters should be kept within reach. It might seem excessive to devote a whole itinerary to these three waterfalls, but they are only revealed in their grandiosity – and 150m drop – once you've checked them out close up. From Lillaz you only get a glimpse. The quiet village where the walk starts has a good choice of cafès and restaurants, hotels, the odd food shop and many drinking fountains.

At the bus stop and car park at Lillaz (1617m) signposting for the cascate sends you across the bridge through the small village. Take the second L through to Bar Cascate and onto a geology trail. The wide track follows the bank of the stream and you ignore a fork R for Lago Loie. It's not far to the foot of the **lower fall** – you climb up through shrub vegetation to good viewing points.

Then iron rungs and handrails help you up rock surfaces to the **middle fall**, with attractive transparent pools. The path then climbs up dry hillsides temporarily away from the falls, to reach a path junction. Close by is a giddy **bridge** over the torrent gushing through a photogenic rock channel.

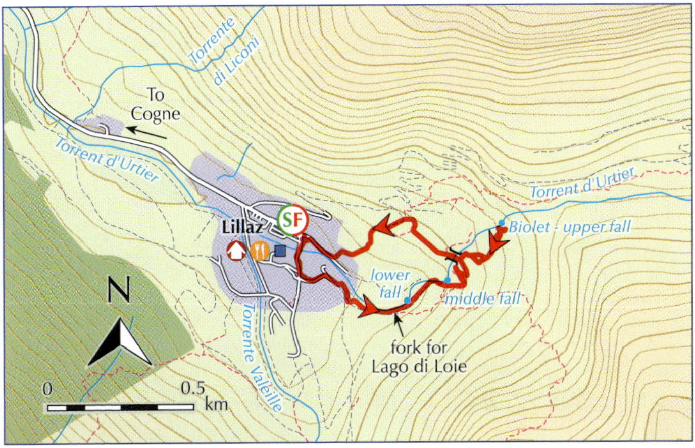

The gushing Lillaz waterfalls

From here continue R uphill past a lookout tower through a flowered meadow where martagon lilies abound. Benches and a good belvedere are perfect for admiring the **upper fall** (Biolet, 1710m) thundering out from a rock cleft.

A narrow path leads down to an idyllic sheltered wooded area of tranquil pools among boulders. Watch your step. Here weary feet can be instantly revived in the invigorating water.

To complete the circuit, go back to the last bridge and keep R. Path n.14 leads between enormous glacially modelled rocks and light woodland to emerge in vegetable gardens on a hillside shrouded in rosebay willowherb. You soon join the main descent path from Vallon de Urtier. It comes out near the stream once more, and not far down the dirt road past a small hydro-electric power station is the bus stop you started from at Lillaz (1hr 30min).

WALK 2

Lago di Loie

Start/Finish	Lillaz bus stop and car park
Time	5hr
Distance	12km
Ascent/Descent	825m
Grade	2
Access	Summer bus from Cogne

This beautiful, if lengthy, round trip in the Vallon di Cogne is suitable for all the family. The only difficulty is the steepish climb in the first part. As well as a variety of landscapes, there are plenty of panoramic points with marvellous views ranging as far as Mont Blanc. The lake area, brightly flowered, is a popular picnic spot and you may well see the herds of chamois that frequent the surrounding mountainsides and crests. During the return descent a detour can be made to take in the magnificent Lillaz waterfalls (see Walk 1).

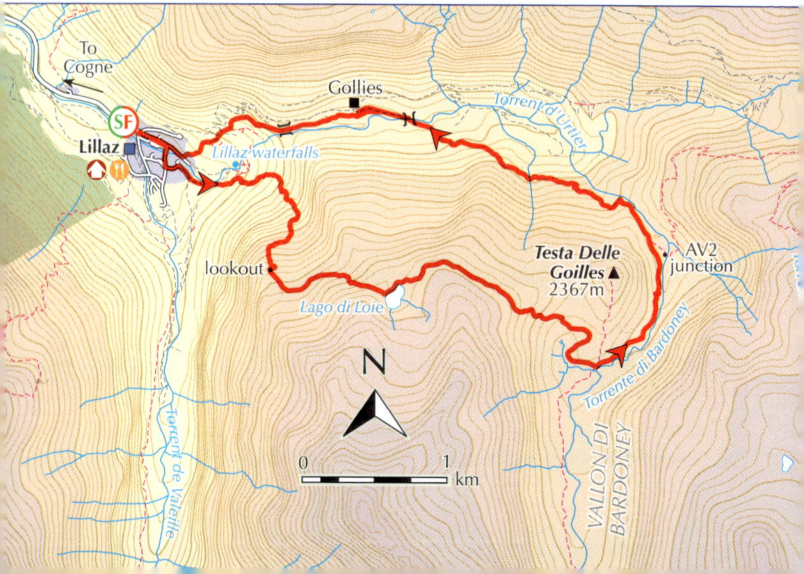

The path climbs away from the lake

From the bus stop and car park at Lillaz (1617m) cross the bridge following signposts for route n.12 into the village. Take the second L to Bar Cascate. Soon after a geological area where the waterfall path continues alongside the stream, n.12 starts its climb R (S). This is one of the few woods in the area and the Arolla pines, larch and fir provide welcome shade while alpenrose, bilberries and wildflowers brighten the undergrowth.

After steady and often steep climbing alongside a trickling waterfall, you emerge onto abandoned pasture near the overgrown ruins of Alpe Loie (2216m). Watching out for marmots, detour briefly R to an excellent **lookout**. In the distance towering beyond Cogne is the Grivola W, while closer at hand is Punta Fenilia SW, not to mention the collection of icy peaks S up the wild Vallon di Valeille.

Above the tree line now, the clear path heads E across rubble for the final uphill stretch across easy open grass and rock terrain. Check the slopes above for solo male chamois at rest at a distance from the herds of females with their young.

Blue-green **Lago di Loie** (2354m, 2hr 15min) nestles in a cup-shaped basin overlooked by grey points such as Punta di Loie (SSW).

The steeply sloping banks of **Lago di Loie** are covered by purple asters and black vanilla orchids, whereas the northern bank consists of glacially smoothed rocks. The area lends itself to picnics and even perhaps a (quick) swim. The name, also spelt Loye, comes from *'lex'* locally used to refer to large slabs of rock used for roofing. Over the Vallon de Urtier are the abandoned mine buildings at Colonna, lofty and distant like a Tibetan monastery.

Path n.12 follows the side of the lake then climbs to another superb viewpoint from where Mont Blanc is WNW. As the path bears E, mostly level, peaks above delightful Vallon di Bardoney come into view, including Torre Lavina with its remnant glacier SE. You descend towards a sea of green and gold vegetation in a shallow marsh. The path circles the wetter parts – beware of tempting but squelchy shortcuts through the cotton grass! Over a rise the path joins the main path along Vallon di Bardoney (45min), a short distance from a summer farm (Alpe Bardoney). The valley has widened considerably here and spells lush green pasture. When livestock are not around, the marmots come out. The name Bardoney means a concentration of Rumex acetosella, otherwise known as sheep sorrel.

The walk enters Vallon de Bardoney on the return stretch

Keep L (NE). The torrent rushes through deep passages before a lovely long drop into a blue pool. Further on is an **AV2 junction**, and from here on you share the path with the long-distance route and its black and yellow triangle. It is NW now zigzagging down through conifer wood alive with song birds. After intersecting a farm track, you cross a wide **bridge** over Torrente Urtier and soon keep L to a path junction below the tiny hamlet of **Gollies** (1854m).

Ups and downs through tall vegetation lead into the narrower lower valley and immense slabs of glacially polished rock with the renowned Lillaz cascate (waterfalls). To see them at close quarters, take one of the branches off L to the bridge (see Walk 1). For the direct descent, keep on the winding path following water pipes down through scrubby wood to the valley floor. A short stretch R past a small hydro-electric power station brings you out at Lillaz (1617m, 2hr) and the bus stop where the walk began.

WALK 3

Vallon de Valeille

Start/Finish	Lillaz bus stop and car park
Time	2hr 50min
Distance	9km
Ascent/Descent	300m
Grade	1–2
Access	Summer bus from Cogne

This is an excellent first walk in the park with gentle gradients. It wanders up a quiet valley on an old game track that is remarkably well preserved. Wildlife sightings are on the cards – marmot colonies dot the slopes and their echoing cries cannot be missed, chamois flit through the trees while hordes of grasshoppers occupy the dry slopes in summer.

A sturdy bridge over Torrent de Valeille leads to picnic spots

From the bus stop at Lillaz (1617m) turn R across the bridge and walk through the village, ignoring the 'cascate' fork L. Continue S past a chapel in a meadow thick with pink bistort flowers. You join a road and pass a camping ground. Soon you're pointed sharp L onto n.15, a lane winding uphill, never far from the cascading Torrent de Valeille which will be a constant companion today. After a quarter of an hour you cross to the R side of the valley on a **bridge** (1687m) – views open

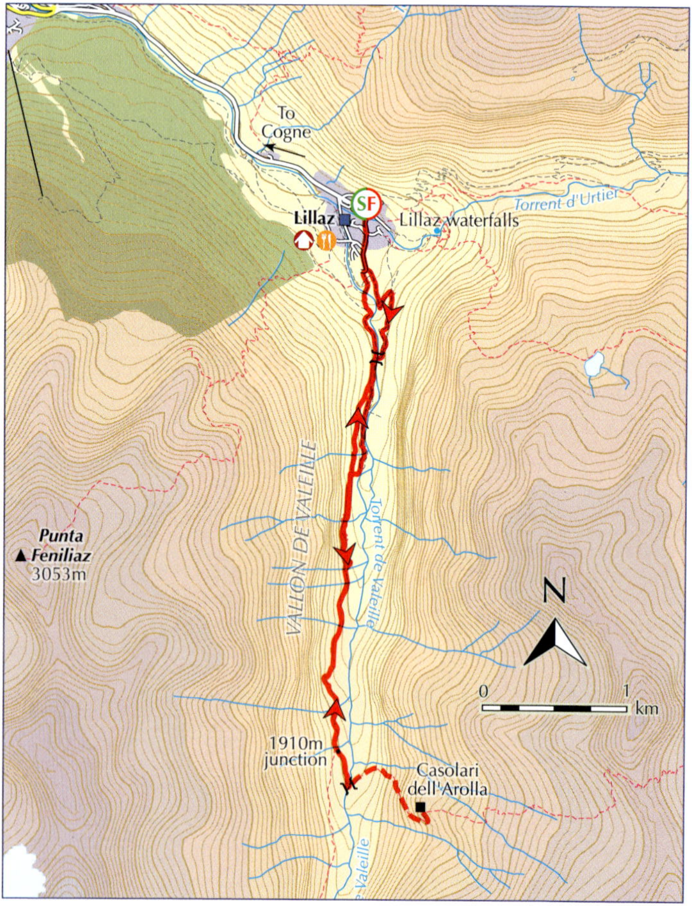

An old game track leads up Vallon de Valeille

up beautifully all the way up to the minor glaciers hanging around rocky towers of Punta delle Sengie. All very promising. Not far on, in the vicinity of an impressive massive angled boulder, don't miss the fork R where n.15 takes an old game track with a perfect gradient and stone reinforcing. Ascending gently above the river, it traverses avalanche chutes and larch wood alternating with open terrain colonised by juniper and alpenrose interspersed with raspberries.

At a **1910m junction** branch L on n.15A to a bridge (1hr 30min) crossing the torrent to inviting picnic spots.

Extension to Casolari dell'Arolla (1hr)

Path n.15A becomes a tougher (grade 3) route as it clambers the outcrop where a Park hut is perched at Arolla (2258m). Experienced walkers only. Watch your step.

Main route

Return the same way you came down Vallon de Valeille to the bridge (1687m). Instead of crossing it, stick to the left bank and go straight ahead on n.15A. At a meadow don't miss the abrupt branch R down through woodland and across the torrent to the camping ground. Walk through to the road and return via the chapel to Lillaz (1hr 20min).

WALK 4

Cascades de Pila

Start/Finish	Gimillan bus stop
Time	2hr 20min
Distance	6.5km
Ascent/Descent	280m
Grade	1–2
Access	Summer bus from Cogne

Not overly taxing, this pleasant straightforward route with some great panoramas leads out of the mountainside hamlet-cum-viewpoint of Gimillan into lovely Vallon de Grauson. Summer farms dot the way as you proceed to the waterfalls Cascades de Pila. While nowhere near as dramatic as the famous Lillaz falls, it's a worthwhile walk destination all the same.

For a longer route that explores the marvellous upper valley and the Lussert lakes, see Walk 5.

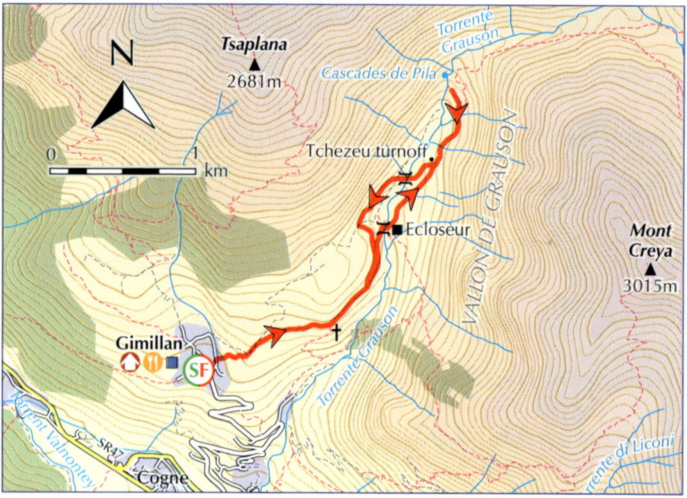

Vallon de Grauson widens marvellously near the Cascades de Pila

From the bus stop at Gimillan (1774m) walk uphill to a fountain then go R to a sizeable batch of yellow signposts. Branch R (NE) on clear path n.8 across meadows and up to join a lane. The path soon resumes, and you walk underneath power lines near giant pylons. The lovely old way is lined with prolific rose and juniper bushes and occasional larch trees. A whitewashed **shrine** marks a junction where you keep straight ahead, running along the precipitous edge of Vallon de Grauson and past a fork (3C, the return route). The way dips across the torrent on a bridge at **Ecloseur** (1910m), an idyllic pasture basin with a modest farm. A gentle climb ensues over terrain dotted with fallen rocks from Mont Creya. Ignore the turnoff L (1969m) for Tchezeu (the return route) and proceed up a flight of rock steps to a signposted fork L for the falls through a sea of juniper shrubs past an old farm. You squeeze around a rock corner to the **Cascades de Pila** (2021m, 1hr 20min), which come crashing down below an impressive outcrop. Watch your step as it gets slippery here. The base is concreted for the water offtake.

A shrine marks a junction in Vallon de Grauson

Until a few years ago, the local farmers and herders diverted water from **Torrente Grauson** through ingenious excavated channels to irrigate their meadows (essential for haymaking to feed livestock) and supply their summer farms. The channels still line the way, but nowadays the water runs through below-ground piping to sprinklers from an offtake at the falls.

Return to the **Tchezeu turnoff** and go R to a **bridge** and nearby farm, then keep L on n.8E. Here the path is flanked by channelling which gushed with water until recently. In woodland, ignore a fork R and you soon rejoin the outward path and branch R. Retrace your earlier steps. As the path emerges onto open terrain, you enjoy fantastic views over to the Gran Paradiso group rife with soaring peaks and glaciers. Continue back to Gimillan (1hr).

WALK 5

Laghi di Lussert

Start/Finish	Gimillan bus stop
Time	6hr 20min
Distance	19km
Ascent/Descent	1200m
Grade	2
Access	Summer bus from Cogne

Beautiful Vallon de Grauson and its lovely high-altitude lakes are not in the national park but make a memorable if rather strenuous day trip entailing considerable height gain. The pastures high and low are still used for grazing, but luckily for walkers, no roads have been put in. Marmots and shy chamois are constant companions high up, in addition to gliding birds of prey.

Paths and waymarking are clear and straightforward. Friendly Rifugio Grauson is a handy stopover and can always be used as an overnight stop should you prefer to stretch the walk out.

From the bus stop at Gimillan (1774m) walk uphill to a fountain then go R to a batch of yellow signposts. Branch R (NE) on clear path n.8 across meadows and up to join a lane. The path soon resumes, passing underneath power lines near giant pylons. The lovely old way is lined with prolific rose and juniper bushes and occasional larch trees. A whitewashed **shrine** marks a junction where you keep straight ahead, along the precipitous edge of Vallon de Grauson and past a fork (3C). It dips across Torrente Grauson on a bridge at **Ecloseur** (1910m), an idyllic pasture basin with a modest farm. You climb gently over terrain scattered with fallen rocks from Mont Creya and ignore turnoffs for Tchezeu and the Cascades de Pila fall (2021m, unless you have time for the 15min detour – see Walk 4).

Flowered terraces dotted with shepherds' huts and larch are followed by a landmark metal cross. Not far on cross the bridge over to **Grauson désot** (2273m) alpage. On the L side of the torrent now the valley widens, with glaciated Punta Tersiva visible ESE and graceful, pointed Grivola in the distance WSW. At a sign-posted junction (2398m), turn abruptly L (N) on path n.8A to friendly log cabin **Rifugio Grauson** (2510m, 2hr 30min).

Punta di Leppe
3305m
Punta del Valaisan
3307m
Punta Garin
3448m
Punta Fleurie
3258m
Mont Grauson
3240m
Pointe Coppi
3231m
Punta di Arpisson
3035m
Tsaplana
2681m
Superiore
Intermedio
Laghi di Lussert
Inferiore
Rifugio Grauson
2510m
Grauson désot
Vallon de Grauson
Torrente Grauson
Cascades de Pila
Ecloseur
Mont Creya
3015m
N
0
1
km
Gimillan
SF
Torrente Grauson
Torrente di Liconi
SR47
Cogne
Torrent d'Urtier

Rifugio Grauson is tucked into the mountainside (photo Wouter Batsleer/Pieter Van den Bulck)

Then proceed N up over hillocks and rises past another farm into the ample green expanse of this peaceful side valley. Vast, flattened and glacially smoothed expanses of rock are crossed while opposite is an invading oversized wall of moraine, bulldozed by the Ghiacciaio di Lussert. When you reach an unmarked junction keep straight on for the lowest and largest lake, **lago inferiore**, beyond the crest at 2721m (45min).

Back at the junction, take the N fork for the second lake. The path, narrower and steeper now, climbs quickly up crumbly loose terrain then follows a ridge. It emerges on the broad shores of the inky middle lake, **lago intermedio** (2800m, 20min). Fed by a trickling stream from the upper lake, it occupies a steep-backed cirque amidst pink-red rock, blackened on the surface – yet another delightful flowered picnic spot.

Charr, a type of alpine trout, survive in the chilly waters of the Laghi di Lussert tarns which occupy armchair-shaped cirques scooped out by an ancient glacier.

For the final stretch to the top lake, follow the yellow arrows right along the shore to where clear marking guides you up rocky walled sides and NW into the next desolate cirque. Snow persists well into summer at this altitude along with resolute gentians, daisies, and yellow-centred violets around the shore of this highest lake, **lago superiore** (2907m, 15min). Only the splash of the occasional fish surfacing breaks the silence. The pronounced peak of Punta Garin stands out WSW.

Return to Rifugio Grauson then Gimillan the same way – allow 2hr 30min.

Lago superiore di Lussert

WALK 6

Montseuc

Start/Finish	Upper station Pulsé telecabina (gondola car)
Time	2hr
Distance	3.6km
Ascent/Descent	330m
Grade	2
Access	From Cogne take the Valnontey road (Rue Grand Paradis) and fork L up Rue Laydetré for the telecabina (10min)

Close to the village of Cogne, heavily wooded Montseuc doesn't attract much attention, yet it is easy to access and offers a rewarding circuit with stunning views up the sweep of Valnontey with its glaciated wonders as well as Vallon Urtier and the old mines set at remarkably high sites. The route is a well-trodden '*Sentiero Natura*' (nature trail) with info panels along the way. Walkers traverse thriving woodland dominated by Arolla pines, which attract noisy nutcrackers intent on gathering as many kernels as they possibly can to store away for the winter. Meticulously emptied pine cones litter the paths in late summer.

In terms of difficulty, it's average with several brief narrow stretches along the upper ridge, as well as some steep ups and downs.

Alight from the gondola car at the upper station (2072m) and turn R uphill to the **cafè**. Here signposts point you R (W) on n.17 through beautiful conifer wood to a marvellous belvedere. Then take a deep breath and follow the yellow arrows carefully to climb steeply SE along the wooded ridge. A number of stunning viewpoints regale more views. But **Montseuc** (2327m) itself, marked by a small cross, is even better and, in addition to the massive glaciated spread of the Gran Paradiso group, takes in majestic Mont Blanc NW, as well as neighbouring Punta Fenilia. The name Montseuc means 'goat without horns' due to its rounded shape as it contrasts to the pointed peaks in the vicinity.

As you continue SE, the ridge narrows a bit then you descend steps L, followed by a lovely traverse through bilberries, alpenrose and larch. Across the valley are the Cogne mine buildings high up on the flanks of Mont Creya. After a winter ski lift on **Grand Crot** (2272m) the marked way descends via a ski slope to a path junction – fork L (NW) on wide track n.17A (Sentiero Natura). Keep your

View up Valnontey from the ridge

eyes peeled for abrupt changes of direction (signed for telecabina) and descents. Knees permitting, in next to no time you'll be back at the cafè and gondola car for the return to Cogne.

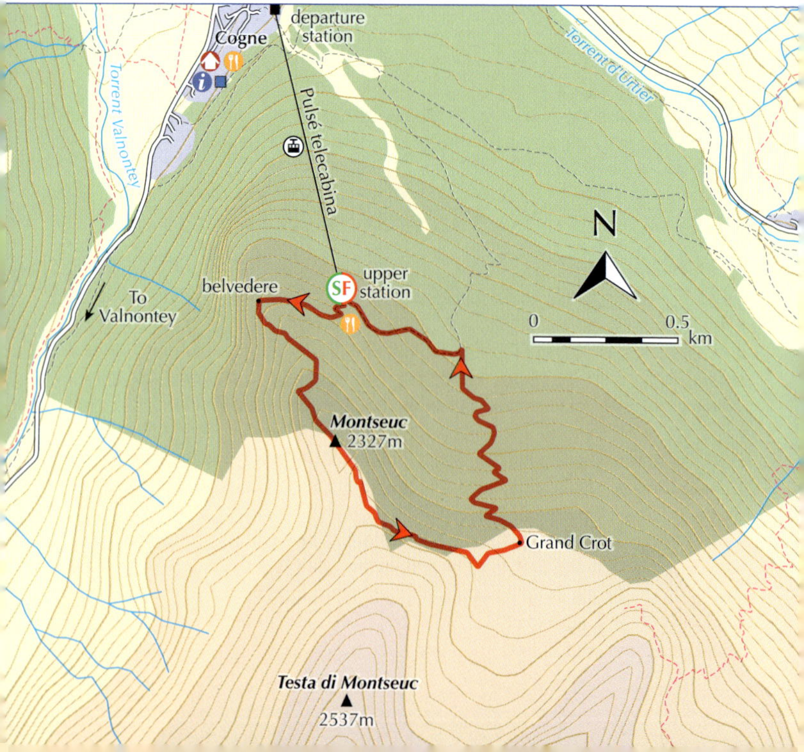

WALK 7

The Money Glacier Terrace

Start/Finish	Valnontey
Time	6hr
Distance	15.7km
Ascent/Descent	815m
Grade	2
Access	Summer bus from Cogne

Though not a stroll, this superb and popular day outing is a perfect first walk for a Gran Paradiso holiday. It is in Valnontey – both the name of the village where the walk starts as well as the valley. Every ounce of effort spent in climbing the 815 steep metres to Alpe Money is fully repaid by the ample magnificence of the cascading Tribolazione glacier beneath the impressive chain of peaks from the Herbetet around to Gran Paradiso and Roccia Viva. Closer at hand it is not unusual to see ibex grazing on the high slopes even in midsummer.

While the opening part of the walk along the floor of Valnontey follows a wide easy track, the ascent to Alpe Money is steep and tiring in places and unsuitable for youngsters. After a superb traverse you then point your boots valleywards and cross a string of streams that become swollen with snowmelt in the afternoon; Park staff install temporary bridges (June–Sept) over most but be aware that getting your feet wet is on the cards. Take special care on especially hot midsummer days, and as an alternative be prepared to retrace your steps from Alpe Money – not that those stream crossings will be dry either!

From the bus stop and car park at Valnontey (1666m) are promising views upvalley of glaciers and peaks, a mere hint of what is to come. A few minutes upstream is a bridge with signposts. Follow n.22 SSW, keeping to the R side of the whitewater Torrent de Valnontey past cafès and hotels. A wide lane passes a camping ground then swerves R over a bridge to resume its direction. Pasture precedes a fork (ignore it) to eatery **Agriturismo Pra-su-Piaz** (1702m) then the lane recrosses the river. It's a leisurely stroll through conifer wood and past clusters of old huts including **Vermiana** (1729m).

Testa del Gavio
3046m
N
0
1
km
To Cogne
SF
Valnontey
Torrent Valnontey
Agriturismo Pra-su-Piaz
Punta Feniliaz
3053m
Bec du Vallon
2837m
Vermiana
Torrente Gran Vallon
n22C turnoff
Pont de l'Erfaulet
Alpe Money
Torrente dell'Herbetet
Torrent Valnontey
2046m junction
Punta Tsissetta
3419m
Punta Patrí Nord
3561m
Torre di Sant'Orso
3618m
Torre del Gran San Pietro
3692m
Becca della Pazienza

Upper Valnontey opens up during the ascent to Alpe Money

After about an hour you reach the **n.22C turnoff** L for the start of the climb. Stiff at times, it is initially a sequence of tight zigzags. Beneath the meagre larch trees are pink alpenrose, wine-red martagon lilies and fresh yellow gentians. At the tree limit you swing around L to the first of several moderately exposed passages with cables, then, after further climbing, the path resumes its southerly bearing to contour across dry mountainsides. The panorama verges on breathtaking but gets even better.

There's a rushing stream to be crossed on wobbly stones followed by ups and downs, then a junction for 'Biv Money' which you ignore and keep on to the pasture of **Alpe Money** (2334m, 3hr). The few abandoned shepherds' huts still standing are on a base of vast grey-brown slabs, lime green with lichen, of glacially smoothed rock – a reminder that the glaciers ahead once submerged the entire valley and ice masses slid along these flanks high up above the present valley floor.

According to legend, a **ghostly horseman** attired in green was once known to appear at Col Money and descend in great leaps and bounds over the glacier to play havoc with the milking cows, as revenge for a young shepherd being treated badly. On a calmer note, the place name is believed to be pre-Roman and is commonly found in Valle d'Aosta as a term for 'shared pastures'. Equivalents reputedly exist in the Irish moin and Gaelic moneth.

Due W over Valnontey are the Casolari dell'Herbetet, below the triangular peak of the same name, while over in the 180° sea of ice the rock protagonist is Gran Paradiso SW.

Now following occasional yellow arrows, embark on n.22D due S with a short climb at first on mixed rock and grassy terrain below the foot of the Ghiacciaio di Money. Not always clear, the path begins its descent towards upper Valnontey

The stunning position of Alpe Money

and includes icy stream crossings. A good halfway down is a steep descent down loose moraine and finally to the valley floor and Torrent de Valnontey again.

On the opposite bank a clear path leads N through scrubby green alder to the **2046m junction** with the path from Casolari dell'Herbetet (Walk 8) – keep R.

Easier and wider now, follow the path along the L bank to cross the sturdy wooden bridge **Pont de l'Erfaulet** (1826m). Not far on is the n.22C turn-off for Alpe Money (2hr); keep straight ahead the same way you came earlier to return to Valnontey (1hr).

WALK 8

The Casolari dell'Herbetet Traverse

Start/Finish	Valnontey
Time	7hr 20min
Distance	19.4km
Ascent/Descent	1100m
Grade	2–3
Access	Summer bus from Cogne

In the ever-popular valley of Valnontey, this route via Rifugio Vittorio Sella to the Casolari dell'Herbetet huts is one of the most spectacular itineraries in the whole of the Gran Paradiso. A rather narrow but well-maintained path runs along the valley's western flank at a dizzy altitude of 2500m, breathtaking panoramas onto the immense glaciers and icefalls improving with every step. The PeakFinder App will come in especially handy today. As if further attractions were necessary, the zone is densely populated with wildlife – approachable ibex, chamois and marmots.

Note: While the traverse itself is not suitable for beginners due to the exposure (and inadvisable for anyone in low cloud or bad weather), the first stage as a return walk to Rifugio Vittorio Sella makes a wonderful family day trip (Grade 2).

Lastly, of great interest close to the walk start is the Giardino Botanico Alpino 'Paradisia'.

A short stroll uphill from the bus stop and car park at Valnontey (1666m), turn R across the bridge as per Alta Via 2/n.18. The asphalt soon ends and a clear path leads past the **botanical garden** to a waterfall with a wonderfully long drop. You head up the mountainside on the easy curves of an old mule track still used by the laden pack horse that plods up to the refuge. Leaving larch wood behind, the path crosses a timber **bridge** onto open terrain dotted with summer farms amidst clumps of edelweiss, not to mention comical colonies of marmots devouring thistles and daisies. Views improve considerably towards the glaciers S. After a second **bridge** where you switch back to the R side of the stream, wide zigzags lead up to enter a vast basin. Here stands an old photogenic hunting lodge, now home to the park rangers. Not far on you come to the former stables transformed

Testa del Gavio
3046m
botanical garden
SF
Valnontey
To Cogne
Torrent Valnontey
Rifugio Vittorio Sella
2679m
Agriturismo Pra-su-Piaz
Punta Feniliaz
3053m
Lago di Lauson
Bec du Vallon
2837m
Vermiana
Torrente Gran Vallon
Casolari dell'Herbetet
Pont de l'Erfaulet
Torrente dell'Herbetet
Torrent Valnontey
N
0
1
km
2046m junction
Punta Tsissetta
3419m
Punta Patrí Nord
3561m
Torre di Sant'Orso
3618m
Torre del Gran San Pietro
3692m

Rifugio Vittorio Sella, once stables for one of the king's hunting lodges

into hospitable **Rifugio Vittorio Sella** (2679m, 2hr 30min), named after the highly acclaimed pioneer mountain and glacier photographer whose black-and-white masterpieces from the late 1800s remain unsurpassed. The rifugio has a homely feel, and walkers are fed well.

Note: before proceeding, check with the rifugio that the ensuing section is safe to follow in terms of stream crossings.

From Rifugio Vittorio Sella head SE on n.18B across the stream and along the winds of the paved game track in gradual ascent across damp grassy terrain and glacially smoothed rock slabs. The waters of picturesque tarn **Lago di Lauson** (2656m, 30min) reflect grandiose peaks and glaciers.

After an easy walk around to the next point, the track comes to an abrupt end and a narrow path begins in brief descent. There is a reassuring, if short, length of chain at the very start, but the following 30min mean ups and downs with longish, moderately exposed stretches, requiring care and attention. Once around the midriff of Bec du Vallon, the path widens to enter the valley dominated by Gran Serra and Punta di Levionaz. After a stream crossing below the remnant Gran Vallon glacier, the path continues S over rubble, guided by cairns. It climbs to a platform at 2600m, a magnificent viewing point where the icy masses of the majestic Ghiacciaio della Tribolazione seem only a stone's throw away SSW. The crest above it is punctuated by the Gran Paradiso peak SW and a host of others.

The path now drops down the escarpment, a very brief narrow passage, to the similarly panoramic **Casolari dell'Herbetet** huts (2435m, 2hr), park property. The name means 'small pasture area'.

The spectacular path below the Casolari dell'Herbetet

The track in descent (n.2G) has come through the ravages of many a winter in excellent condition, and its well-graded curves and built-up corners make it a delightful and relaxing walk. It snakes its way towards the valley floor a giddy 400m below. The air is heavy with the thundering of waterfalls from the semicircle of ice at the head of Valnontey.

The path turns decidedly S to avoid a steep cliff and into the welcome shade of larches, down to a bridge then a path **junction** (2046m) where you veer L. The going is easier and wider now. Through an unusual profusion of green alder shrubs mixed with conifers, you wind down to cross the wooden bridge **Pont de l'Erfaulet** (1826m). On the R torrent bank you stroll past groups of old huts such as **Vermiana** (1721m). A short stretch on the L bank passes a short detour to cafè **Agriturismo Pra-su-Piaz** before you recross the river to reach the campsites, hotels and cafès of Valnontey (2hr 20min) once more.

WALK 9

Punta Pousset

Start/Finish	Cretaz
Time	7hr 30min
Distance	13.7km
Ascent/Descent	1570m
Grade	3
Access	The village of Cretaz lies 1.5km N of Cogne, on the year-round bus line from Aosta.

The name for extraordinarily panoramic Punta Pousset comes from the French '*poucet*' meaning thumb, as that is what it resembles when seen from the Cogne valley. Perhaps the first mountaineers to record their visit, Yeld and Coolidge, writing in 1893, called it 'the Gornergrat of Cogne'. The wide-ranging views are unbeatable but there the resemblance to the Swiss peak ends, luckily, as neither the cogwheel train nor the floods of tourists are to be found here – the only crowds likely en route will be the wildlife – sizeable herds of chamois as well as ibex in upper Vallone del Pousset.

The route is straightforward until the stretch of crest leading to the actual peak. This section is not a Sunday stroll and is suitable only for expert walkers. Experience on exposed terrain and rock and a sure foot are essential. You need a good dose of stamina to deal with the hefty climb and a picnic lunch with plenty of liquid refreshment. Weather-wise a perfect, cloudless day – and no wind – are best. Last and not least, an early start is vital.

From Cretaz (1494m) cross the Grand Eyvia and take marked path n.25. It climbs steeply W through wood and pasture and crosses a stream to the groupings of huts known as **Les Ors** (1944m, 1hr).

Continue SW and at a **2170m junction** fork R onto n.25C that leads N onto the ridge separating Vallone di Vermiana from Vallone del Pousset. You climb past a **Casotto PNGP** (park ranger's hut, 2289m, with a tap) then drop to Torrente de Pousset. You join n.26 here and the path heads W criss-crossing the stream before climbing up to a vast area of glacially polished rock. After a wooden cross are the old huts of **Pousset dessus** (2520m).

Punta Pousset has an unmistakable shape (photo Wouter Batsleer/Pieter Van den Bulck)

Above the buildings then you resume W proceeding over grassy terraces where herds of chamois graze. A good way up, at the next marked **junction** (2818m, 2hr 45min), leave the path for Bivacco Gratton and instead take the R branch for Punta Pousset.

It curves its way N, cutting across the steep grassy flank at the head of the valley, zigzagging up to emerge at a minor col. Watch your step. Follow yellow arrows carefully and clamber up a rock face and an open chimney leading to the crest. A series of rock slabs and exposed ledges and an aided stretch need negotiating carefully on the last leg to the rocky point and summit cross of **Punta Pousset** (3046m, 45min). Breathtaking panoramas await. As Yeld and Coolidge put it, 'Cogne is at your feet', not to mention what appears to be the whole of the Alps as well.

Return the same way to Cretaz (1494m) and allow around 3hr.

The dizzy rocky top of Punta Pousset looking over Cogne (photo Wouter Batsleer/Pieter Van den Bulck)

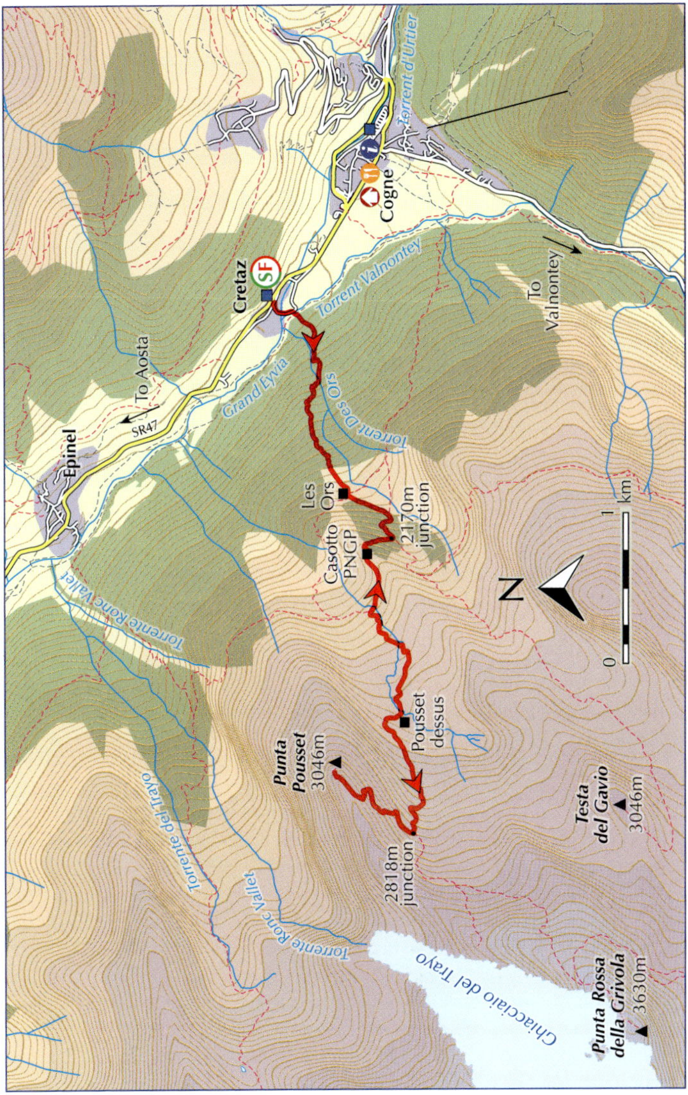
Cogne
Cretaz
Epinel
Torrent d'Urtier
Torrent Valnontey
To Valnontey
To Aosta
SR47
Grand Eyvia
Torrent Des Ors
Les Ors
Casotto PNGP
2170m junction
Torrente Rone Vallet
Pousset dessus
Punta Pousset 3046m
2818m junction
Torrente del Trayo
Testa del Gavio 3046m
Punta Rossa della Grivola 3630m
Ghiacciaio del Trayo
N
0
1
km
SF

WALK 10

Beneath the Grivola

Start	Epinel
Finish	Vieyes
Time	6hr 30min
Distance	12.5km
Ascent	1440m
Descent	1710m
Grade	2–3
Access	Both Epinel and Vieyes are served by the year-round Aosta to Cogne bus.

The centrepiece of this awesome route is a 'beautiful maiden', the Grivola, a magnificent pointed peak first scaled in 1859 by a group of British climbers guided by a local game warden. The best viewing point is the Alpe Gran Nomenon in the second part of the itinerary. Second in magnificence if not fame is its elegant neighbour Mont Gran Nomenon, which towers over the eponymous valley. For the geologically-minded, the Grivola is composed of calcareous schist with ophiolites in contrast to the metadiorites that make up the Gran Nomenon.

The walk is pretty quiet and challenging, with long ascents and descents, rating average on the difficulty scale. Expect late-lying snow around 2875m Col du Trajo in early summer.

From the sports ground in the lower part of Epinel (1465m) take the wide bridge across Grand Eyvia. Follow signposting for path n.27, an unremitting climb SW beneath conifers, their needles soft underfoot. It's a good hour to the cableway and huts at **Pianes** (1686m). Keep R and across the stream up diagonally and the path soon emerges onto an open slope, to bear R across a rubble gully in the shade of Punta Pousset with promising glimpses of the upper valley. A stretch of larch wood and several stream crossings on, over a rise is **Trajo** (2040m, 1hr 30min). Also spelt Trajoz or Traso, the name refers to a route followed by shepherds with their livestock. These picturesque stone-slab-roofed houses built in timber that has weathered to a rich red-brown look NE to Monte Emilius. One has been converted into a comfortable dortoir Lou Mayèn de Léne.

To Aosta
F Vieyes
SR47
Plan Pessey
Torrente del Grand Nomenon
Grand Eyvia
2756m
Punta Monpers
2793m
Punta della Valletta - Vetta scialpinistica
3007m
N
0
1
km
Torrente Arpisson
Petit Nomenon
Epinel
S
Torrente del Trayo
Pianes
Bivacco Gontier 2315m
Alpe Gran Nomenon
Casotto PNGP
Trajo
Grand Eyvia
SR47
Torrente Ronc Vallet
Col du Trajo 2873m
To Cogne
Grand Nomenon
3488m
Punta Pousset
3046m
Torrent Des Ors
Ghiacciaio del Trayo

Back on the main path, keep climbing to the **Casotto PNGP** (2150m) set in a panoramic clearing. Above the tree line now you climb around an old moraine ridge of the diminutive Grivoletta glacier. Soon a steep rocky flank and yellowish rock gully require some effort. This climb emerges onto a flattish pasture basin with a small lake, home to chamois. The final leg is not as steep, although late-lying snow is possible. **Col du Trajo** (2873m, 2hr 30min) finally opens up between Punta Crevasse and Punta di Trajo, but it is of course the towering Grivola that attracts attention.

Casotto PNGP above Trajo

The descent (n.5D) zigzags due W at first down a stony slope where the path is not always clear. It terminates in a beautiful grassy basin with a trickling stream at the base of the imposing Grivola pyramid. Joined by another path an easy stretch R (N) drops to the **Alpe Gran Nomenon** with its refurbished huts, another Casotto PNGP and cosy **Bivacco Mario Gontier** (2315m, 1hr). This cosy stone and timber chalet is anything but 'unalluring' as Yeld and Coolidge described it a century ago, although they did acknowledge the 'unrivalled position'. Here the Grivola can be enjoyed from yet another viewpoint, together with its brother Gran Nomenon SW, not to mention the wide-ranging views to the N of the snowcapped ridges beyond Aosta.

Yellow arrows for n.5 wander N down the hillside. Cross to the R side of the stream and drop past a derelict hut to a bridge at **Petit Nomenon** (1987m, 30min).

Soon in a wood of silver fir where cushions of rare twinflower grow, the path winds pleasantly downwards. The valley narrows and you cross L beneath an impressive waterfall where laden thickets of raspberries line the path.

The next landmark is **Plan Pessey** (1375m), a traditional medium-altitude farm. Go diagonally L here into tall dense forest. The path curves easily down along old stone terracing on the final stretch and comes out on the road near a bus stop across from the quiet hamlet of **Vieyes** (1114m, 1hr 30min), whose few remaining inhabitants desert it during the sunless winter months. In addition to drinking water, it offers visitors a small frescoed church.

The elegant Grivola looms over the descent route

IBEX

Ibex are at home here, but an encounter with the giant 'ibex king' is the stuff of legends. Renowned as a sort of devil who uttered incomprehensible languages and kidnapped young children, his reputation was 'enhanced' after a challenge from the valley's fearless Hunter King. The encounter was brief as the hunter, blinded by bogus superiority, lost his footing and hurtled down a ravine. In contrast, an enormous golden eagle, erstwhile resident of the Grivola, was renowned for his humanitarian qualities. According to an ancient legend the local people, tired of suffering intense cold and mists, turned to the eagle for help. Eyes blazing, he set dead trees alight and thus introduced man to fire and heat.

OVERNIGHT ACCOMMODATION

With a little advance organisation to book and collect keys, a memorable overnight (self-catering) stay is feasible either at Trajo (Dortoir Lou Mayèn de Léne loumayendelene@gmail.com tel 340 0024155 key at Epinel) or Grand Nomenon (Bivacco Gontier tel 338 1771841 key at Aymavilles).

WALK 11

Pont d'Ael's Roman Bridge

Start	Pont d'Ael (aka Pondel turn-off)
Finish	Aymavilles
Time	2hr + extra for visiting the bridge
Distance	6km
Ascent	160m
Descent	420m
Grade	2
Access	Alight from the Aosta-Cogne bus at the Pondel turn-off, 4km above Aymavilles

The great attraction of this walk is a marvellously intact, two-storey Roman bridge-cum-aqueduct, an astounding 50.5m long and 2.20m wide.

The walk entails several narrow stretches and is mostly downhill. A torch can be reassuring for the short tunnel.

From the bus stop (906m) and signposted turn-off on the main Cogne road, it is a quiet walk down to the hamlet of **Pont d'Ael** aka Pondel (890m, 15min), possibly derived from *'ponticulus'* small bridge. Arrows guide visitors through the maze of houses to where the bridge spans the river at a height of 61.5m. Via the ticket office you can visit the covered passage with a dizzy glass floor (Apr–Oct) for a modest fee, while the top level is always open and free; water flowed here over sealed rock slabs.

PONT D'AEL AQUEDUCT

The aqueduct was built in 3BC to carry the unusual combination of water, people and goods across a deep gorge. A toll was charged for pedestrians and livestock using the covered lower passage while the top level was an aqueduct. The water was channelled down the westernmost bank of the Grand Eyvia from Chevril, 3km upvalley. Traces of the excavated channels, originally 1–1.5m wide and 1.5–2m deep, are still visible along the rock face, although the suspended sections have disappeared. The water supply was destined for the quarry of grey-blue marble near Aymavilles, used to construct the Roman city of Aosta no less.

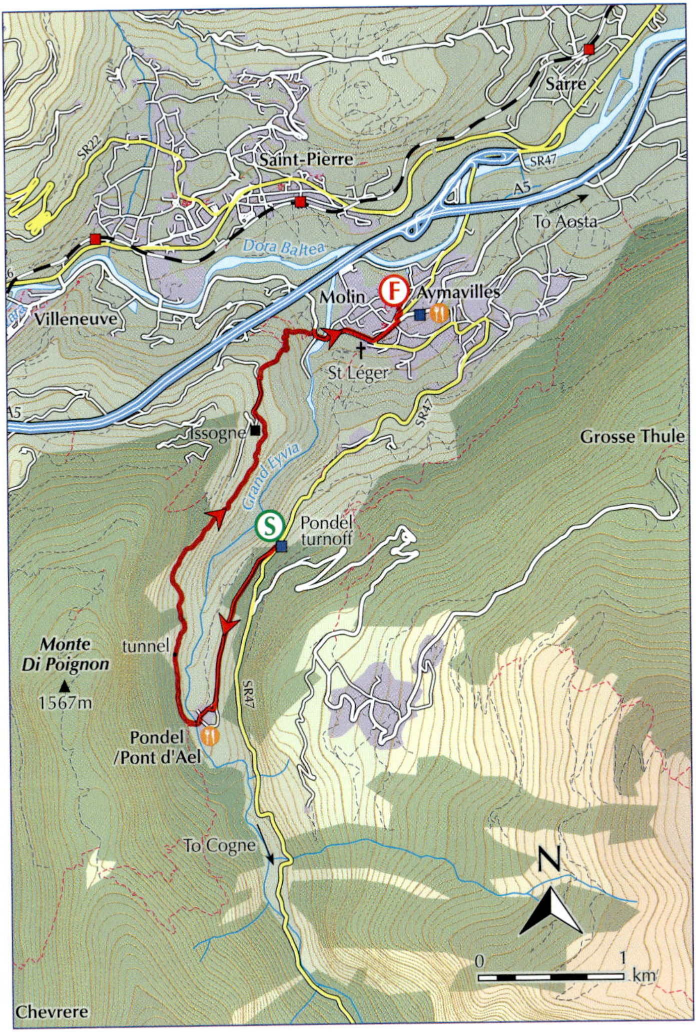
Sarre
Saint-Pierre
SR22
SR47
A5
To Aosta
Dora Baltea
Villeneuve
Molin
Aymavilles
St Léger
Issogne
Grand Eyvia
SR47
Grosse Thule
Pondel turnoff
Monte Di Poignon
1567m
tunnel
Pondel /Pont d'Ael
SR47
To Cogne
N
0
1
km
Chevrere

The marvellous Roman bridge

According to the keystone inscription, Caius Avillius Caimus, a private entrepreneur from Padua, had the bridge built at his own expense; the nearby village of Aymavilles is named after him. Pondel on the other hand was once an important Roman stronghold against the local Salasso population who were holding out further up the Cogne valley.

At the far end of the bridge, fork R on path n.2A heading N, high above the river. It follows stone terracing once home to vineyards. The dry terrain is now the domain of crickets and butterflies. As well as snow-capped ridges visible NE beyond Aosta, there are good views back to the bridge, backed by the distant Grivola.

After quarter of an hour of imperceptible ascent is a seemingly impassable rock barrier where you enter a 60m-long **tunnel** excavated by WWI Austrian POWs (who are also to be thanked for the Cogne road). It does have a window but a torch is useful.

The path zigzags down the steep flank then resumes its N direction and can feel a little exposed. After a bridge and path junction, keep R. Crumbly side gullies are crossed on wooden bridges and you may surprise chamois in the woods. You emerge to green fields and an old rambling farmhouse at **Issogne** (850m).

The old WW1 tunnel

The villa-cum-castle at Aymavilles, the walk end

Turn R below the buildings and through to the road where signs for n.2A point you R twice down a lovely old path lined with stone walls and chestnut trees alive with scavenging squirrels. As you round the hillside past a shrine on the edge of the main Aosta valley, the fanciful turrets of the 11th-century castle of Saint Pierre appear ahead. Manicured vineyards precede a road – turn R across the bridge and up past the hamlet of **Molin** and its flourishing orchards. Keep on the main road below the church of **St Léger** with its curious 18th-century trompe l'oeil frescoed façade.

Go L at the intersection to **Aymavilles** (641m, 1hr 45min) for bus stops, shops and cafès, in the shade of its curious villa-cum-castle.

WALK 12

At the Foot of the Gran Paradiso

Start	Pravieux
Finish	Pont
Time	6hr
Distance	14.5km
Ascent	1180m
Descent	1040m
Grade	2
Access	Valsavarenche is served by buses from Aosta all year round as far as Eaux Rousses, extending a further 5km to Pont in summer. Pravieux is midway between Eaux Rousses and Pont.

This excellent problem-free route in Valsavarenche is a rather long haul but includes a superb high-altitude traverse with sweeping panoramas.

Wild animal sightings are guaranteed as huge numbers of ibex inhabit these flanks. The most popular section is the Pont–Rifugio Vittorio Emanuele II path, while the traverse itself is relatively untrodden.

GRAN PARADISO SUMMIT

The route connects two important and popular rifugi, both essential bases for mountaineers heading for the Gran Paradiso. At 4061m and the only peak wholly within Italian territory that exceeds 4000m, its first recorded ascent was by English climbers JJ Cowell and W Dundas with French guides Michel Payot and Jean Tairraz in 1860. In this day and age, the ascent enjoys enormous popularity, consequently an overnight stay in either of the rifugi usually means being woken at an ungodly hour as groups set out for the summit!

Near the bus stop at Pravieux (1829m) follow signposting for path n.5 and Rifugio Chabod, over a wide bridge. You veer S past characteristic vaulted farm buildings, to where a masterpiece of alpine path construction awaits – a mule track with carefully built-up corners climbs in regular curves E, keeping to the L of a cascade, out of sight. Livestock have been escorted to summer pastures along this route for centuries. The conifer wood is alive with squirrels and nutcrackers.

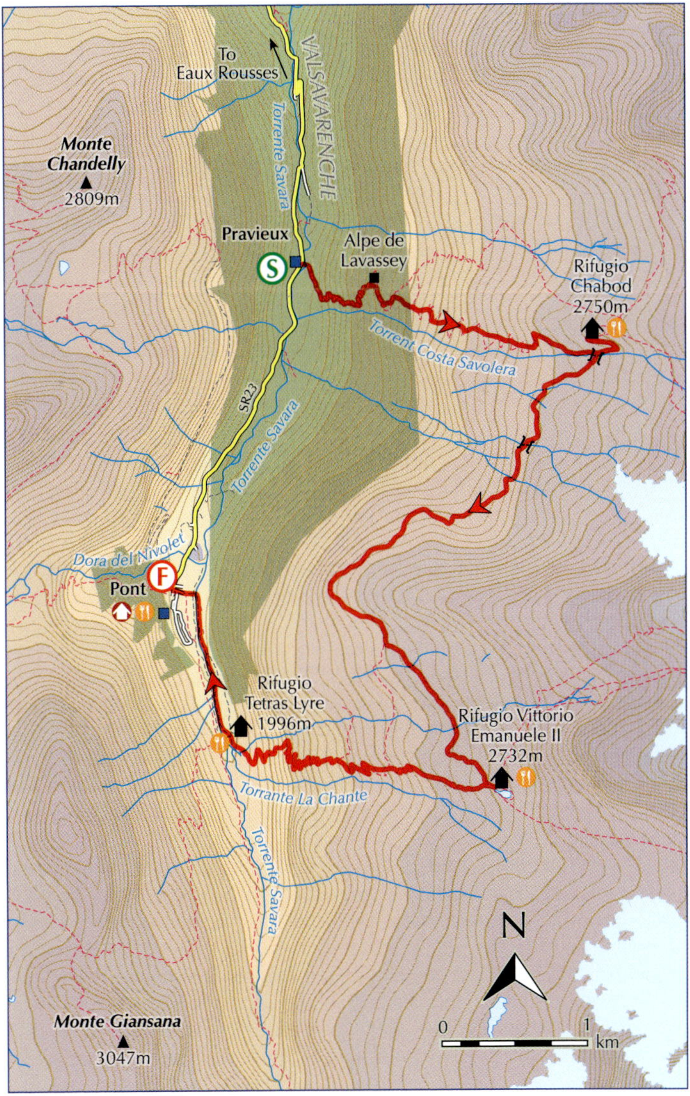
To
Eaux Rousses
VALSAVARENCHE
Torrente Savara
Monte Chandelly
2809m
Pravieux
S
Alpe de Lavassey
Rifugio Chabod
2750m
Torrent Costa Savolera
SR23
Torrente Savara
Dora del Nivolet
F
Pont
Rifugio Tetras Lyre
1996m
Rifugio Vittorio Emanuele II
2732m
Torrante La Chante
Torrente Savara
N
0
1
km
Monte Giansana
3047m

Vast glacier-smoothed rock slabs after Rifugio Chabod

At 2194m is a clearing with the modest farm **Alpe de Lavassey**. There are ample views of the opposite flanks of Valsavarenche, right up to Punta Basei SW. Keep R at the path junction (ignore n.5A to Bivacco Sberna). As the larch trees thin, immense expanses of glacially smoothed rock come into sight, often with ibex standing sentinel on the crests. Fawn-coated chamois graze on the grass flats, ready to flee at any hint of danger.

After a good few hours winding and plodding, well above the tree line, you pass a wooden **bridge** (2643m, n.1A turns R here for the traverse – by all means take it to if you prefer to skip Rif Chabod) and shortly afterwards is the rifugio's turbine at the base of a cascade. A wide path climbs diagonally L up the final 100m to a platform and **Rifugio Chabod** (2750m, 2hr 30min). It occupies a simply magnificent position facing the northwestern flank of the Gran Paradiso, Piccolo Paradiso and dominant Becca di Montandayne. The modern but simple rifugio was named after a local inhabitant who became the first President of the Valle d'Aosta's autonomous government following WW2. Hours can be spent observing the large herds of ibex that hang out on the rock slabs on the opposite bank of the torrent.

Return to the wooden bridge and cross it L (SW) for path n.1A in gradual descent SW. Spreads of moraine are encountered below the retreating Laveciau glacier, the name for a place where salt would be left for animals. After a second **bridge** over a tumultuous freezing cold stream you face a series of ups and downs as you round the Testa di Montcorvé then cross a desolate stone-filled valley.

Back on grass once more, at a path junction, take the L branch for the final climb. (The wider track straight ahead joins the descent path.) You climb over smoothed rock slabs then meagre pasture punctuated with gentians and oxeye daisies.

Rifugio Vittorio Emanuele II (2732m, 2hr) stands just back from a small tarn, Moncorvé. The position is superb. Virtually due S is slender pointed Becca di Monciair, while SE is the rounded form of La Tresenta and the impressive north wall of the Ciarforon is SSE.

The original **rifugio**, now used as an annexe, was inaugurated in 1884 in honour of the Hunter King and at the cost of 6160 lire. Writing in 1893, Yeld and Coolidge described it as 'very commodious (5 rooms) and very well fitted up in all respects, so that it is probably the best Club hut in the Western Alps, and has therefore been named "The Palace"'. The popularity of this area and the Gran Paradiso ascent made a more spacious building necessary. The decision was taken in 1927 but work (partially funded by the Marshall Plan) wasn't completed until 1961! The hangar-like metallic building is rather incongruous but it sits well among the moraine.

For the descent a clear well-trodden track (n.1) heads W downhill. Glacially smoothed and lichen-stained rock slabs dominate. The easy path allows time to enjoy the vast landscape and views over Valsavarenche. Late afternoon will guarantee an encounter with the laden pack mules that supplement the rifugio's start-of-season helicopter drop of foodstuffs.

After endless curves the path enters a larch wood with bilberries and alpenrose. You reach the valley floor near cosy **Rifugio Tetras Lyre** (1996m) close to the torrent. Then it's a final stroll R (N) along to the bridge crossing for **Pont** (1960m, 1hr 30min) and the bus stop, enormous car park, campsite, shop, as well as hotels and restaurants scattered down the road.

The awesome position of Rifugio Vittorio Emanuele II

WALK 13

The Gran Collet Circuit

Start/Finish	Pont
Time	4hr 30min
Distance	11km
Ascent/Descent	870m
Grade	2
Access	Pont is served by summer buses, an extension from Eaux Rousses and the year-round line from Aosta.

This itinerary in upper Valsavarenche wastes no time heading up to the spectacular Gran Collet pass where views are incomparable and the Gran Paradiso close at hand.

Afterwards you drop via the Pian del Nivolet before returning to Pont via landmark wooden cross La Croix de l'Arolley. While the walk is not particularly difficult, the climb is steep and relentless, requiring good stamina. Be aware that the high pass may be blocked by snowdrifts well into the summer. The circuit sees few walkers but plenty of animals – do take care not to disturb the herds of chamois and ibex and their young.

From Pont (1960m) and the car park walk through to the river but don't cross the bridge. Turn R on the lane along the bank up Vallone di Seyvaz. Quarter of an hour along at the fork L for **Rifugio Tetras Lyra**, you need the narrow path that breaks off R, marked by a yellow 2A. The climb is immediately stiff and the path narrow but good. Bearing almost imperceptibly SSW it heads for abandoned **Alpe de Seyvaz** (2364m), now home to marmots and a Casotto PNGP. At the head of the valley the Grand Etret glacier is visible, overshadowed by the Denti del Broglio.

Continue S a little longer before veering W to climb through a series of grassy basins, many occupied by ibex females and their inquisitive young who spy on visitors. Iron rung steps and short rods help you up abrupt rocks.

At the last ample terrace preceding Gran Collet, a photographic stop is called for if you haven't already exhausted the possibilities – from the pass itself the view is partially obscured. From ESE to NE is the stunning sweep taking in Ciarforon,

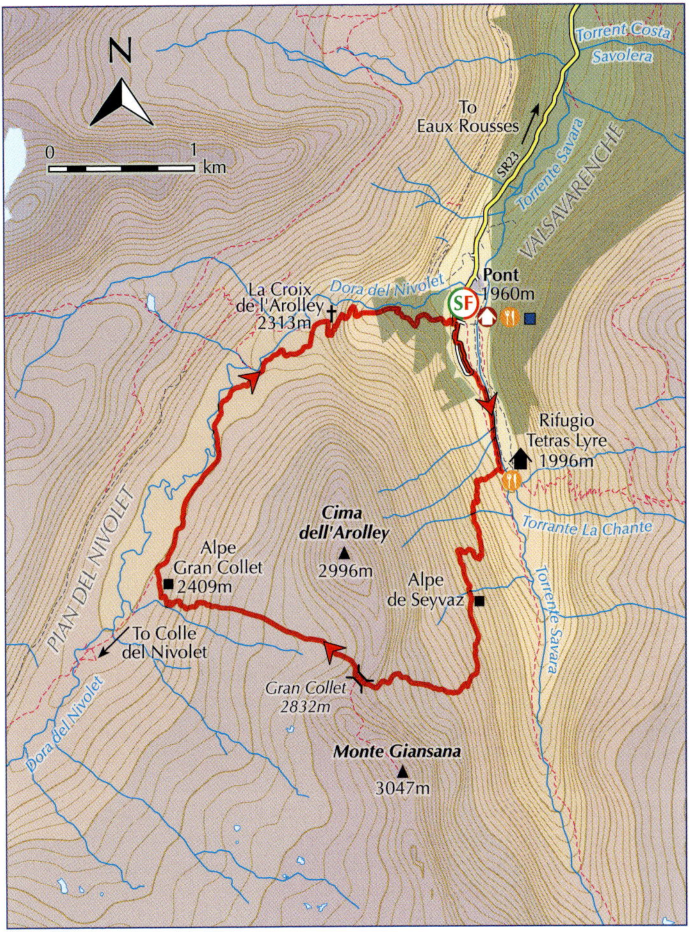

Tresenta, the shiny metal roof of Rifugio Vittorio Emanuele II beneath Gran Paradiso, then Piccolo Paradiso and Becca di Montandayne.

The last leg cuts up to the ample saddle of **Gran Collet** (2832m, 2hr 30min), where a squawking flock of alpine choughs awaits crumbs. Interesting new views

The stone skeleton huts of Alpe Gran Collet

range over the ample Pian del Nivolet dominated by Mont Taou Blanc and Punta Basei interspersed with glacier and snow pockets.

This extensive **altopiano** lying 2300m to 2500m above sea level is an ancient glacial valley where silt transported by water has accumulated over time, resulting in fertile grasslands, appreciated by rotund grazing cows and sheep.

Now you head WNW down a dirt slope and back onto grassy terrain bejewelled with blue gentians and riddled with marmot burrows as well as tarns. Where the path as such disappears, cairns point the way down to the Pian del Nivolet, where you turn R in the vicinity of the stone skeleton huts of **Alpe Gran Collet** (2409m, 40min).

Landmark Croix de l'Arolley

In the open valley, n.3 rambles NE alongside a gushing stream and marshy terrain dotted with flowers. Brief ups and downs lead over expanses of polished rock and there's an abundance of inviting picnic spots.

After a path junction is the prominent old wooden cross **La Croix de l'Arolley** (2313m). Then you plunge E in zigzags on a reinforced path down a steep escarpment to a waterfall. Larch and alpenrose accompany the rest of the way to Pont (1960m, 1hr 20min).

WALK 14

The King's Path in Valle delle Meyes

Start/Finish	Pont
Time	5hr
Distance	13km
Ascent/Descent	830m
Grade	2
Access	Pont is served by summer buses, an extension from Eaux Rousses and the year-round line from Aosta.

High above the western flanks of Valsavarenche, this circuit walk ascends to solitary Valle delle Meyes then heads along one of the most panoramic stretches of royal game track in this northern part of the park. The sweeping views embrace a magnificent line-up of mountains including the Gran Paradiso in its snow and ice setting. Wildlife sightings are on the cards as eagles, ibex, chamois and marmots hang out up here.

No particular difficulty is involved in this walk and it's suitable for energetic family groups. A torch is handy for the short tunnel in the opening section.

At Pont (1960m), a short distance downhill from the main car park is the start of a wide surfaced track off L, marked n.4. After several wide curves, it heads decisively N to a short tunnel. Further along at a second tunnel (2192m) where the road veers L, take the path straight ahead (n.4). This heads up diagonally L to a shrine near old farm huts (**Meyes Dessous**, 2278m). The view E across the valley to the Gran Paradiso and surrounding peaks and glaciers is nothing less than breathtaking, but it improves!

A bit of history: the initial 3km of the **ascent track** was part of an access road for the purposes of a late 1960s hydroelectric project which, unlike a string of others, never materialised due to environmental concerns, thankfully leaving the valley quiet and untouched. The road was to link Valsavarenche with Valle Orco in the south via Colle del Nivolet.

Now turn L on n.6/6A, a broader path climbing SW in wide curves past more huts before reaching the especially picturesque huddle at **Meyes Dessus** (2542m) which blends in perfectly with its rock-lichen surroundings.

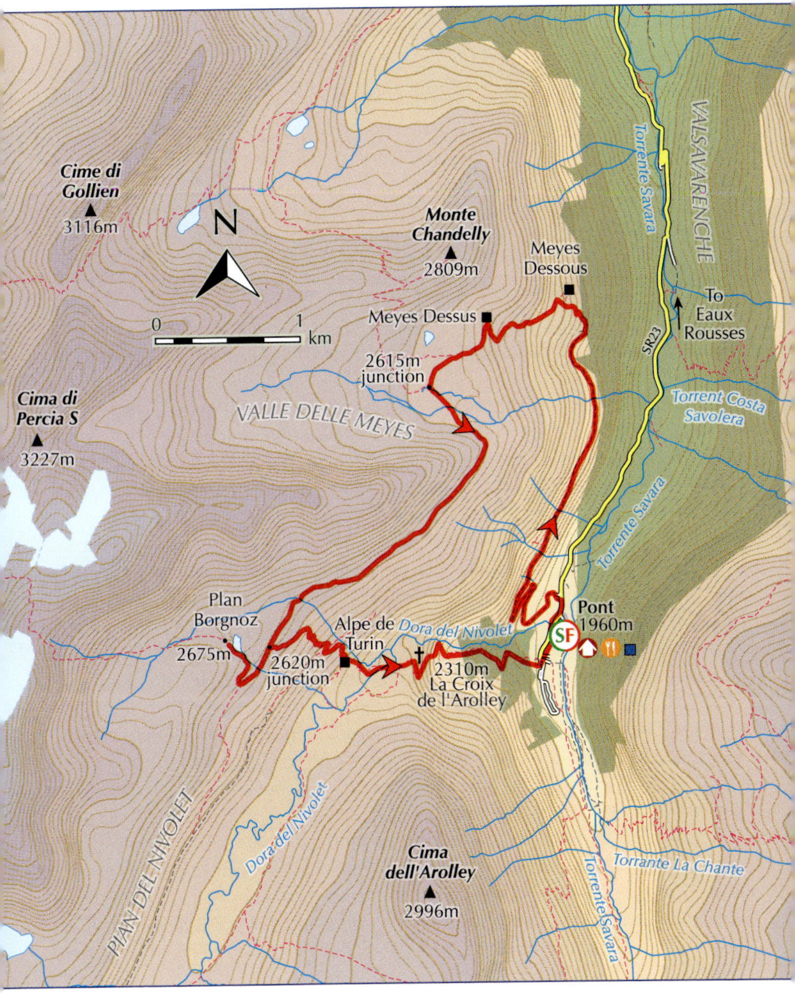

The Meyes Dessus huts blend into the rock surrounds

A series of glacially shaped steps lead on to Valle delle Meyes, where your passage will undoubtedly send marmots shrieking and scampering in all directions. At the foot of the imposing Manteau ridge is a signposted **junction** (2615m, 2hr 10min) near a small lake. Branch L to join the king's hunting track (n.9) in this little-frequented desolate valley where birds of prey hang out. Above is the moraine left by the Ghiacciaio di Percià.

You are led through squelchy boggy flats thick with cotton grass and across a stream on stepping stones. Gentle uphill SE at first on a marvellous stretch of paved track sees you round the rock bastion Costa des Aouille – probably a reference to 'eagle'. Around the corner is a lookout point par excellence high over deep U-shaped Valsavarenche with the Herbetet, Gran Paradiso... out with that PeakFinder App!

The path continues its gradual climb to enter another high-altitude marshy flat soaked by meltwater streams from glacier pockets glimpsed around Mont Taou Blanc (named for the whitish-yellow rock). Check the ridges above for chamois. A small tarn precedes stepping stones over a stream. Not far on, neat mounds of rocks from pasture clearing announce a signpost and path **junction** (2620m, 1hr) where the descent route to Pont breaks off L. However, keep straight ahead for a brief but brilliant side trip. At the nearby fork, go R up past a Park ranger's hut and curious vaulted farm buildings to **Plan Borgnoz** (2675m) a silted-up glacial tarn, a marvellous spot and needless to say, with a breathtaking outlook that stars the Gran Paradiso.

Plan Borgnoz is a perfect place for admiring the Gran Paradiso

Backtrack to the 2620m junction (30min) and turn R decisively downhill on n.3A. A well-kept path, it winds valleywards between dry stone columns-cum-oversized cairns. Flights of stone steps lead quickly to a dirt road at 2485m, an extant stretch of the abandoned project. You cut straight across it – signposted n.3 for Pont. Continue down towards the abandoned huts of **Alpe de Turin** (2388m) but just before them, take the path fork L. Near cascades it crosses a clearing with profusions of spotted gentians beneath power lines and crosses a wooden bridge. You join n.3, the main Pont-Colle del Nivolet track (keep L) not far from an old wooden cross in a commanding position. A local reference point, **La Croix de l'Arolley** (2310m, 40min) derives its name from the Arolla pine.

From here the path drops E in a series of tight zigzags with built-up corners, passing a waterfall then entering larch wood with alpenrose and juniper shrubs. You emerge on the valley floor road only a couple of metres from your starting point at Pont (1960m, 40min).

WALK 15

Orvieille and Lacs de Djouan

Start	Dégioz
Finish	Eaux Rousses
Time	5hr
Distance	15.5km
Ascent	1025m
Descent	885m
Grade	2
Access	Dégioz and Eaux Rousses in Valsavarenche are on a year-round bus line from Aosta.

This rewarding walk follows another royal game track to the old Orvieille hunting lodge before continuing up to a batch of picturesque tarns. It traverses woodland and grassed mountain flanks with wide-reaching views and good chances of spotting wildlife.

Quite a hefty ascent of over 1000 metres is involved, however, you can always shorten it to 600m by limiting the walk to Orvieille. The descent route drops to Eaux Rousses but you can backtrack to Dégioz.

From the bus stop and Albergo Parco Nazionale at Dégioz (1547m), take the road downhill (W) and across the bridge over Torrente Savara to the hamlet of Vers le Bois. Marked as n.8, the old game track strikes out NNW at first through wood. Wide easy curves then head SW gradually leaving the trees behind and moving into pasture. The grassy flat of **Orvieille** 'old alpage' (2168m, 2hr) is the site of a marvellous old hunting lodge, now park property. It once hosted royal parties and encampments, and even boasted a telegraph line. The views from here embrace many Valsavarenche peaks as well as a glimpse of imposing Gran Combin far away N, but things improve as you climb.

Heading S now follow the fence alongside the buildings where there is drinking water. It's uphill to a summer farm where you'll probably have to pick your way through a muddy livestock feeding area.

In common with AV2 now, you continue past typical stone-roofed huts and wooden crucifixes on slopes thick with carline thistles and marmot burrows. As

Rovenaud
To Aosta
Torrente Savara
SR23
Punta di Bioula
3414m
Punta Furchin della Bioula
2965m
Punta Bianca
3427m
Vers le Bois
Degioz
Tignet
Le Creton
Torrente di Levionaz
Orvieille
Monte Roletta
3384m
Bien
Torrente di Chaud
Maisonnasse
Eaux Rousses
VALLON DE NAMPIO
0
1
km
Lacs de Djouan
Monte Chandelly
2809m
To Pont
VALSAVARENCHE

Looking downhill from the Djouan tarn (photo by Andrew and Lucie Price)

the trees are left behind the outlook opens up to include Gran Paradiso and the elegant pointed Grivola. You effortlessly enter the Vallon de Nampio, bright with bilberry shrubs and the odd larch, and gain the first of the peaceful tarns, **Lacs de Djouan** (2518m, 1hr 15min). A perfect picnic spot. Apart from wild ducks and alpine charr, herds of chamois and ibex can usually be admired on the surrounding crests.

Return to Orvieille (2168m, 45min) and branch R on n.8C aka AV2. It plunges SE mostly through pasture, woodland and abandoned terraces. Near the valley floor you drop past a trickling waterfall over rust-coloured rock that explains the name of the hamlet of Eaux Rousses (1667m, 1hr). Past a cluster of houses and the Hostellerie du Paradis guesthouse-restaurant you reach the main road and a bus stop.

Peaceful Lac de Djouan backed by Col Entrelor (photo by Andrew and Lucie Price)

Note: It's 3.2km back to Dégioz. If there's no bus handy, walk carefully N along the road and take the lanes that keep L of the tarmac. 40min should suffice back to the start point.

WALK 16

The 2205m Mont Blanc

Start/Finish	Rhêmes-Saint-Georges
Time	5hr
Distance	12km
Ascent/Descent	1025m
Grade	2
Access	Rhêmes-Saint-Georges in Val di Rhêmes has year-round buses from Aosta

Close to the northernmost opening of Val di Rhêmes this modest Mont Blanc is easily 'scaled' without ice-axe or crampons – unlike its celebrated namesake on the Italian-French border. Its isolated and commanding position gives it sweeping, virtually uninterrupted views over the Valle d'Aosta taking in the spectacular 4807m Mont Blanc to Grandes Jorasses line-up, the Grand Combin, the Grivola and Gran Paradiso, to mention but a few.

Walkers can generally count on the access tracks being clear of snow as early as May and as late as November due to its extended exposure to the sun. The first stretch is an easy path which becomes a wide dirt track, making it feasible for anyone who can manage the climb of 1025m! Added attractions are the stable colony of ibex around the peak and a good chance of sighting chamois in the woods.

A short distance uphill from the bus stop at Rhêmes-Saint-Georges (1159m), take the turn-off for Coveyrand. The narrow asphalt road climbs NE to the hamlet's Ecole Maternelle school in a small square and car park at 1234m. Head uphill on the road, which soon becomes a dirt track closed to unauthorised traffic. Not far on you turn R at a prominent fork. (Champromenty and Mont Blanc are signposted to the L along the road, a much lengthier variant.) Now you follow the path (n.4) through light vegetation and across a stream, cutting up through bird-filled conifer forest and climbing steadily. It intersects the road three times before reaching picturesque summer farm **Mayen de Champromenty** (1813m), complete with a characteristic stone-slab roof, turret and drinking water. No-one should expect shepherds to live in uninteresting places and the outlook here is simply

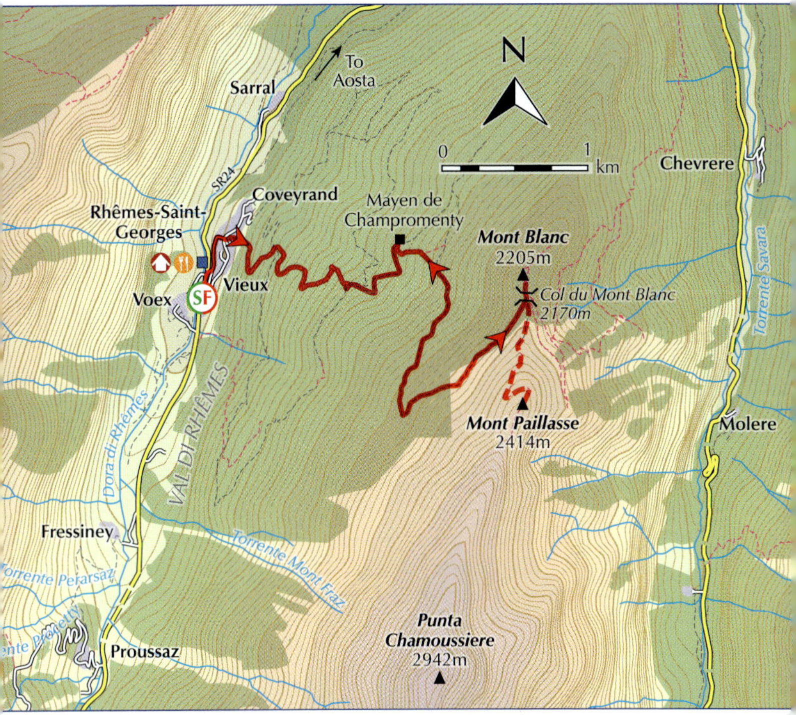

wonderful: although 'limited' to the Val di Rhêmes, the view takes in pointed Becca di Tey, the Grande Rousse and neighbours.

In this area the **dialect** designation mayen means a medium-altitude farm that can be utilised as early as May to provide the livestock with fresh grass while waiting for the snow to melt on the higher altitude pastures – where the huts are known as montagnes.

Now continue up the wide farm vehicle track (still n.4), swinging S then NE. There are thick banks of pink alpenrose beneath thinning larch, a meagre cover for the shy chamois who usually betray their presence by dislodging stones. The views open up gradually as you head towards a modest mount due N with a distinctive light colour.

At Champromenty

At the wide saddle of **Col du Mont Blanc** (2170m) leave the track and head for the Casotto PNGP. Just before it, take the path L around the rocky outcrop. After a grassy slope and then a short scramble, you are on the highest point of breathtaking **Mont Blanc** (2205m, 3hr). Out with that PeakFinder App! The view ranges virtually uninterrupted from W to ENE (taking in Mont Blanc) then resumes SE with the slender sharp points of the Gran Nomenon and Grivola, followed by Gran Paradiso and Ciarfaron.

This lower **Mont Blanc** owes its name to the light colour of its calcareous rock. The walk used to be a jealously guarded local secret but this changed after Pope John Paul II came here during one of his Valle d'Aosta summer sojourns.

Extension to Mont Paillasse (1hr 20min return)

For those with extra energy to burn, an even more extensive outlook can be gained in exchange for a further 250m (45min) in ascent. From Col du Mont Blanc, rejoin the track and proceed S along the wide grassy ridge then up to the top of 2414m **Mont Paillasse** and its trig point.

Main route

Return the same way to Rhêmes-Saint-Georges (2hr). A feasible variant is to take the road down from Champromenty. It does make for a more leisurely descent if a fair bit longer, however be aware that it is surfaced a good part of the way.

WALK 17

Vallon di Sort and Vallon di Entrelor

Start/Finish	Bruil, Rhêmes-Notre-Dame
Time	4hr 30min
Distance	9.2km
Ascent/Descent	850m
Grade	2
Access	Bruil is the main settlement of Rhêmes-Notre-Dame, and it has year-round buses from Aosta.

In beautiful Val di Rhêmes, this loop itinerary climbs the little-visited side valley Vallon di Sort before traversing an easy saddle to drop into the vast and more popular Vallon di Entrelor, where it joins Alta Via 2. Wildlife sightings, chamois and marmots in particular, are pretty much guaranteed as well as fascinating concentrations of unusual alpine flowers. The curious name Rhêmes probably comes from *remma* or *rame*, branch or beam in French, a reference to the valley's old timber industry.

Opposite the church in the small square of Bruil, Rhêmes-Notre-Dame (1723m) take the lane cutting E through the old houses and over the river. With AV2 way-marking a path leads up off the road, signed for Entrelor/Sort. Walk past buildings and up into trees, to an **1850m junction** beneath the curious rock formation Le Château Quelet. Here you part company with AV2 and fork L (n.9), marked for Col du Sort. The wood is lovely, larch mostly but interspersed with Arolla pines which are alive with noisy nutcrackers. Underfoot are red cowberries, alpenrose and slender martagon lilies. The trouble-free path heads due E as it climbs into vast silent Vallon di Sort, in the cover of trees all the way to the beautifully positioned **Casotto PNGP** (2294m, 1hr 30min, drinking water). The imposing mass of Grande Rousse W dominates the landscape now; don't forget to scan the nearby ridges for chamois.

Keep R on a wide track (n.7 now) continuing SE towards a stream and marmot colonies. In the vicinity of a large wooden pole keep an eye out for the junction R for Vallon di Entrelor. You climb up to the ruined huts of **Montagna di Sort** (2448m), well below a glacially shaped landscape with well-preserved moraine crests.

N
0
0.5 km
VALLON DI SORT
Casotto PNGP 2294m
Montagna di Sort 2448m
Col Gollien 2560m
Testa di Entrelor
2580m
Plan de la Feya 2403m
VALLON DI ENTRELOR
Rifugio delle Marmotte 2143m
1850m junction
Dora di Rhêmes
To Chavaney and Aosta
Bruil
Rhêmes-Notre-Dame
SR24
VAL DI RHÊMES
Dora di Rhêmes

A fainter path SW climbs over rock marked by the occasional cairn and yellow mark to the ample 2560m saddle **Col Gollien** (1hr) that connects the Sort and Entrelor valleys. From the lowest point of the pass, cross the grassy slopes in the direction of a cairn where yellow waymarks indicate a decisive veer R (SSW). A clear path appears and leads down the side valley to cross a stream. After a stretch beneath a rock outcrop and old stone walled enclosure, a brief climb brings you out at the barrel-roofed huts of **Plan de la Feya** (2403m, 30min).

You have now entered the beautiful Vallon di Entrelor. This is a haven for herds of chamois and ibex. Wildflowers here provide spectacular splashes of colour for the impressive backdrop of the Grande Rousse.

Back on AV2 now, the descent path NW is well-trodden and, after a series of wide curves down to the stream, keeps to its R bank. After an optional turn-off (to nearby Entrelor, 2143m and friendly **Rifugio delle Marmotte**) you reach the verge of the valley and veer R for the descent through conifer wood and a good lookout for the magnificent Granta Parei. You finally drop past the 1850m junction where the ascent route branched off, and return to Bruil (1723m, 1hr 30min).

The **National Park visitor centre** at nearby Chavaney (1.5km) is worth a visit for its enormous stuffed lammergeier, or bearded vulture, one of the last specimens from the times when people were paid to shoot them. It is a precious chance to examine this gigantic bird at close range.

Approaching Rifugio Marmotte (photo by Andrew and Lucie Price)

WALK 18

Rifugio Benevolo and Lago Goletta

Start/Finish	Thumel
Time	5hr
Distance	13km
Ascent/Descent	860m
Grade	2
Access	Bruil (Rhêmes-Notre-Dame) can be reached by year-round bus from Aosta, however you need a car or taxi for the final 4km to the walk start at Thumel.

This is a hard walk to beat. Starting out in beautiful Val di Rhêmes, on the western confines of the Gran Paradiso Park, it takes in a rifugio then a beautiful glacial lake, the icing on the cake. Apart from the popular stretch as far as Rifugio Benevolo, these paths do not see many walkers. Once away from the hut, you find yourself in wild desolate valleys edged with inspiring and sobering seas of ice.

Mid to late summer is the best time to go to ensure snow cover is at a manageable minimum. Overall the walk is of average difficulty, with hefty ascent/descent.

From the large car park near the small farming community of Thumel (1886m, restaurant-cafè), unauthorised traffic can proceed no further. Set out on foot up the jeep track (n.13) and where it curves R, take the wide path straight ahead S. Clearly signposted for Rifugio Benevolo, it is also referred to as the 'Pison' route, possibly from the name of a local avalanche.

The delightful old paved path follows the R bank of the cascading Dora di Rhêmes torrent, and is ablaze with alpine flowers such as willow gentians and pink orchids. The backdrop is the unmistakable towering Granta Parei from *grande parete* or great wall; it fills the valley head and is illuminated to perfection in the morning.

You join the jeep track (2113m) in the vicinity of a waterfall that soaks slow passers-by! A photogenic stone bridge **Ponte Romanico** leads to the other side of the main torrent. Here the path cuts the curves of the track, climbing up a steep

Becca di Giasson
3205m
Becca di Fos
3457m
To Bruil, Rhêmes-Notre-Dame
Truc Blanc
3405m
VAL DI RHÊMES
Dora di Rhêmes
Punta Bassac Nord
3496m
Thumel
1886m
Grande Traversière
3496m
Punta Bassac Sud
3461m
Ponte Romanico
Soches
Lavassey
Pointe Lavassey
2772m
Rifugio Benevolo
2287m
Punta
ssac Deré
3356m
Lago Goletta
2699m
Punta della Paletta N
Punta della Paletta S
3024m
Ghiacciaio di Golettaz
ITALY
cca della
aversière
337m
Granta Parei
3387m
Ghiacciaio di Tsanteleina
RANCE
N
0
1
km

Stepping stones cross Lago Goletta

flank to huts at **Lavassey** (2229m) before finally clambering out onto the natural platform hosting **Rifugio Benevolo** (2287m, 1hr 30min from Thumel). Named after an entomologist from Torino, this hospitable old-style hut is run by qualified staff who know the area like the back of their hand, and it scores high on catering. A regular diner is the sleek fox who hangs around in the hope of scraps.

From the rifugio follow waymarking (n.13D) W down and cross a **stone bridge**. An easy path climbs diagonally NW to the old farm buildings of **Soches** or Sauches (2316m), the spelling depending on which map you have. Here it's sharp L (S). You ignore a turn-off for the Granta Parei lake and keep R up the steep zig-zags to the crest where there are magnificent views to the Gran Paradiso. This leads SW into the stone desert plateau, Comba di Golettaz, following cairns along the L bank of a stream. Below the triangular point of the Granta Parei S, the wrinkled surface of the Ghiacciaio di Golettaz forms the uppermost banks of grey **Lago Goletta** (2699m, 1hr 30min). An otherworldly spot, frequented solely by enormous grey ravens.

The main route returns down to Rifugio Benevolo (1hr) and Thumel (1hr).

The Granta Parei is the star of upper Val di Rhêmes

WALK 19

Lakes above Pian del Nivolet

Start/Finish	Rifugio Savoia bus stop and car park
Time	2hr 30min
Distance	6.6km
Ascent/Descent	260m
Grade	2
Access	Summer bus from Ceresole Reale

This simply superb route visits a good ten of the attractive lakes nestling in the glacially modelled basins above the Colle del Nivolet pass and overlooking the Pian del Nivolet. No great climbs or descents are involved, it's more a matter of wandering through a gentle rolling landscape and enjoying amazing views to the great Gran Paradiso peak itself, as well as a host of other standout mountains. Picnic spots beckon, especially on the lakesides where trout watching makes an enjoyable pastime.

From the bus stop at Colle del Nivolet (2534m) facing Rifugio Savoia go L uphill past the buildings on a path marked with yellow arrows.

Modest Rifugio Savoia where the walk begins

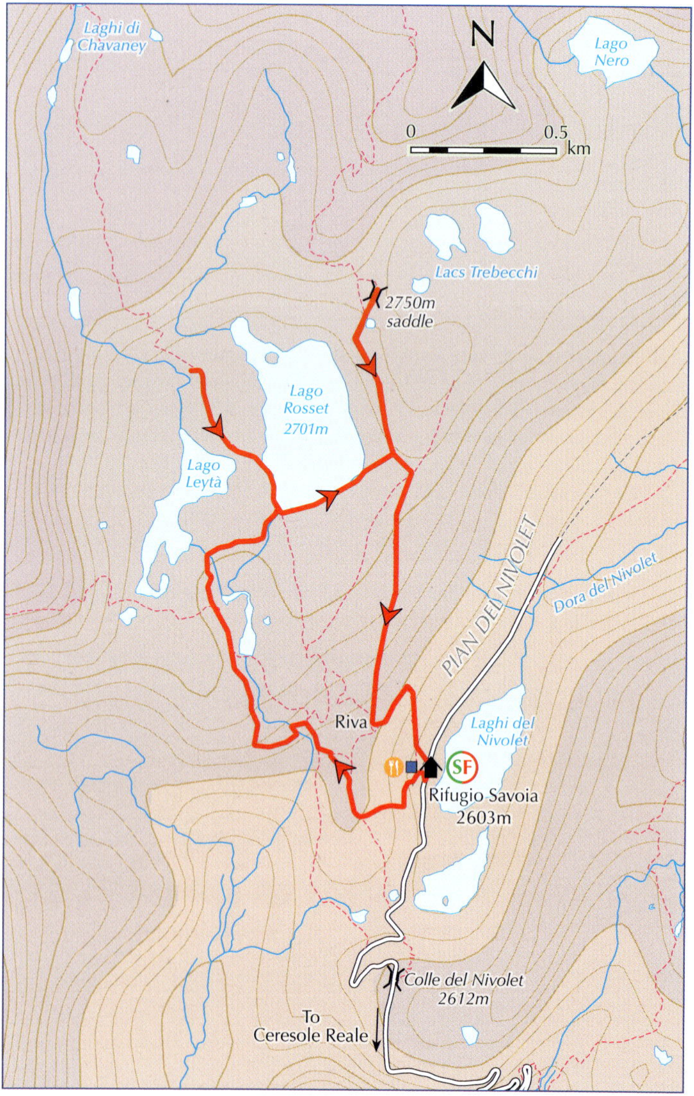
Laghi di Chavaney
Lago Nero
N
0
0.5 km
Lacs Trebecchi
2750m saddle
Lago Rosset 2701m
Lago Leytà
PIAN DEL NIVOLET
Dora del Nivolet
Riva
Laghi del Nivolet
SF
Rifugio Savoia 2603m
Colle del Nivolet 2612m
To Ceresole Reale

The farm above Colle del Nivolet looks towards Punta Basei

It's a gentle climb SSW at first over flowered slopes, up to join a wider path (3C) – turn R. Here you enjoy a decent view to the glaciated Gran Paradiso peak. Not far on, ignore two consecutive forks R to a farm, keeping straight ahead to curve L at the base of a waterfall. Continue N into a trough with elongated lakes, passing a turn-off (n.536) for Punta Basei which comes into view with its modest glacier. A stream crossing close to Lago Leytà then a rise are all that separate you from beautiful **Lago Rosset** (2701m, 45min).

PIAN DEL NIVOLET

The extensive Pian del Nivolet is an ancient glacial valley where silt transported by water has accumulated over time, transforming it into fertile grasslands appreciated by rotund cows and sheep. The altipiano is renowned for the unrivalled spectacle in early summer when ranunculus and pasque flowers transform it into a sea of white and yellow.

At its southernmost extremity is the Colle del Nivolet road pass and access to the southern Piedmont flanks of the park. Thankfully a link road from Valsavarenche proposed in the 1960s related to a hydroelectric project never materialised, leaving the vast peaceful plateau for the enjoyment of livestock, marmots, walkers and other wildlife.

Crossing the outlet of Lago Rosset

Stick to the L bank for the time being along the narrow strip of land separating the two lakes and walk up to the knoll for magnificent views the entire length of **Lago Leytà** backed by the twin points of Punta Galisia and Punta Basei. (By all means proceed further uphill to the Laghi di Chavaney (2846m) at the foot of Col Rosset – allow at least a further 40min – not included in the walk total.)

Return to the start of Lago Rosset (2701m, 15min) and go L via the stepping stones and stick to the shore. The clear unmarked path leads ENE at first. Where the lake shore veers due N, leave it to head E over grassy slopes to pick up marked path 3B due N. The outlook is simply glorious. There's an especially good viewpoint from a knoll high over the head of vast Lago Rosset. After a minuscule tarn you reach a **saddle** (2750m, 45min) overlooking the delightful cluster of the four Lacs Trebecchi backed by the Gran Paradiso no less!

Now backtrack S on 3B following the yellow arrows all the way to the summer dairy farm **Riva** (2621m). Here a wide track drops in wide curves down to Rifugio Savoia and the two adjacent Laghi di Nivolet and the bus stop where you began (45min).

WALK 20

The Royal Track to Ceresole Reale

Start	Bus stop Colle del Nivolet
Finish	Ceresole Reale
Time	8hr
Distance	24km
Ascent	1080m
Descent	2100m
Grade	2–3
Access	The road from Ceresole Reale is open late May–mid October and buses serve it in summer.

One of the best walks in this guide, this marvellous mammoth route of average difficulty follows the most extensive surviving lengths of the original 1800s mule track constructed for the royal hunting parties. You enjoy sweeping views and adventurous walking in desolate rugged landscapes with very few other human beings but plenty of wild animals. Loose rock and earth prevail, providing meagre yet still attractive pasture for both chamois and ibex.

If this route looks too daunting, opt for more manageable Walk 22.

Note: An early start is obviously essential, and extra time should be allowed for unclear waymarking, collapsed stretches of path and snow cover. It is inadvisable to set out on the route in uncertain weather. Not to be underestimated are the mist and low cloud which make orientation decidedly difficult, and which are typical of these valleys.

Go well equipped with food and water as no refreshment points are encountered.

From the bus stop just below Colle del Nivolet (2612m) take the path cutting up S to **Rifugio Città di Chivasso** to join the old game track. It leads SE past a small lake before winding down to shortcut the road, its wide curves supported by built-up stonework. Views are breathtaking high above the dammed Agnel and Serrù lakes, and looking over upper Valle Orco to the crest with Cima del Carro and the Tre Levanne pyramids.

On the roadside near the **Laghi di Losere** (2464m), a signpost marks the start of wide track n.550. It soon rounds Costa della Civetta before going due E, practically parallel to the valley floor on a long panoramic level stretch with stone paved sections and stream crossings.

After scattered stone huts, ignore the path fork at **Alpe Comba** (2497m) that goes R to Chiapili Superiore. Keep L to begin a steady steep climb towards the first pass. The setting is an immense amphitheatre where walkers are mere dots against vast rubble slopes, traversed on wide zigzags.

Ciarforon
3642m
La Torre
3225m
Becca di Monciair
3545m
Torrente Savara
Piccola Torre
3077m
Punta Foura
3411m
Testa del Grand Etret
3203m
VALLON DEL ROC
2274m junction
Alpe Foges
Colle della Porta
3002m
Lago Lillet
Colle della Terra
2905m
Alpe Loserai di Sotto
Colle Sia
2274m
Canale di Manon
Ca Bianca
SP50
SSP460
Rio Crusiè
Ceresole Reale
F
PNGP Visitor Centre
Lago di Ceresole
dam
Rio della Fossa
Rio Plan Pesse
Rio del Dres

Rifugio Città di Chivasso

WEATHER FAIRIES: GOOD & BAD!

Storms in the area are reputedly caused by wind imps letting loose cloud masses at their will then setting off thunder and lightning. The good news is that the whereabouts of Colle del Nivolet have long been renowned for the presence of the ephemeral White Dames, pale robed creatures who flit across steep mountainsides and through avalanches to pluck out unfortunate mountaineers.

Colle della Terra (2905m, 2hr 30min) is a wide saddle separating modest Punta Rocchetta and the crest descending from Mare Percia, with its 'pierced' peak. The landscape changes dramatically now with high walls sheltering the milky-blue lake below; ahead E is Colle della Porta.

The tight zigzags that lead downwards have collapsed in places, easily bypassed, and attractive **Lago Lillet** (2765m, 20min) in its glacial cirque is soon reached. Despite the high-altitude desolate setting, hardy alpine toadflax and chamois cress bloom here

Past the lakeside the path reappears and climbs gradually E in restful curves. Minor peaks La Cuccagna and Cima di Courmaon separate the path from the main valley now. N.550 follows an old moraine ridge and keeps R, avoiding a snow field. A final curve L and you are at **Colle della Porta** (3002m, 50min), the 'door' opening onto an ample wild basin in the shade of Testa del Gran Etrèt.

Head down the often snow-covered slope, sticking with the vestiges of the track as it winds down the immense rubble-filled valley. You are led into the upper Vallon del Roc, below an imposing semicircle of peaks. At about 2700m as a series of streams is crossed, ignore the turn-off for Bivacco Giraudo and head decidedly down R in zigzags to a fertile marshy platform overlooking huts. The path disappears for a while but you're guided by cairns and waymarks and ford an icy torrent. Another path from Bivacco Giraudo joins up, and soon down R the wide track resumes, leading to a **2274m junction** (1hr 40min) above the ruined huts of **Alpe Foges**.

Here you need to leave n.550 and veer R on n.542. A spread of roches moutonnées close off a marshy basin soft with cotton grass. Ibex and chamois share these pastures with the odd herd of cows. Heading S now, the wide level track passes **Alpe Loserai di Sotto** (2210m), a sizeable settlement comprising picturesque stone houses featuring intricate construction techniques. The track climbs a little in wide curves to **Colle Sia** (2274m, 1hr).

Long stretches of the old track are paved

The descent finally starts in earnest and drops S down a bare hillside to more buildings. At the 1998m mark you fork R onto the GTA route to a clearing with scenically sited **Ca' Bianca** (1942m). Now it's decisively SW into a tall conifer wood with woodpeckers. You glimpse the Ceresole Reale dam wall but it never seems to get any closer! Raspberry thickets and laburnum announce the proximity of a dirt road and a park signpost. Close-by is the main road and **Ceresole Reale** (1612m, 1hr 40min). The village

Gorgeous Lago Lillet

is spread out along the road with bus stops, accommodation, shops, tourist office and park visitor centre.

The village probably owes its name to 'cherries', whereas '*reale*' (royal) was added in 1862 by King Vittorio Emanuele II, in exchange for concession of hunting rights for chamois and ibex. It is a peaceful place, with no tales of devils or evil doings, only fairies who leave gifts hanging in trees.

WALK 21

Lago Serrù Sentiero Glaciologico

Start/Finish	Bus stop below Lago Serrù dam wall
Time	2hr
Distance	4.6km
Ascent/Descent	160m
Grade	1–2
Access	A summer bus from Ceresole Reale drops you off below the dam wall where there's a car park.

A fascinating and straightforward circular route in an inspiring setting. It was conceived by experts and ice buffs to encourage visitors to observe glacier-related phenomena. This *sentiero glaciologico* (SG, glacier path) steers well clear of ice and crevasses, following the banks of Lago Serrù, a natural lake enlarged for hydro-electric purposes in the late 1940s.

Marmots and a brilliant array of midsummer wildflowers add to the walk's attraction. There's a modest *glaciomuseo* (glacier museum) at the walk end.

The bridge over the gushing ice-melt stream from Pian Ballotta

From the bus stop at Lago Serrù (2275m) walk past the toilet block and over the wooden bridge. Then, near the foot of the awesome dam wall, turn L on the SG route marked red/white, crossing smoothed rock slabs. Not far up keep L on n.532 across a stream to a fork. Now go R on n.529 to buildings on a level with the top of the dam wall (2292m). There are inspiring views SW to the moraine ridges and the Ghiacciaio della Capra surmounted by Cima d'Oin. Cross the helicopter landing pad L to where red/white markings resume as you enter a marvellous amphitheatre crowned by peaks and rock walls, and hosting several waterfalls. Pink alpenrose shrubs brighten the grassy-rock

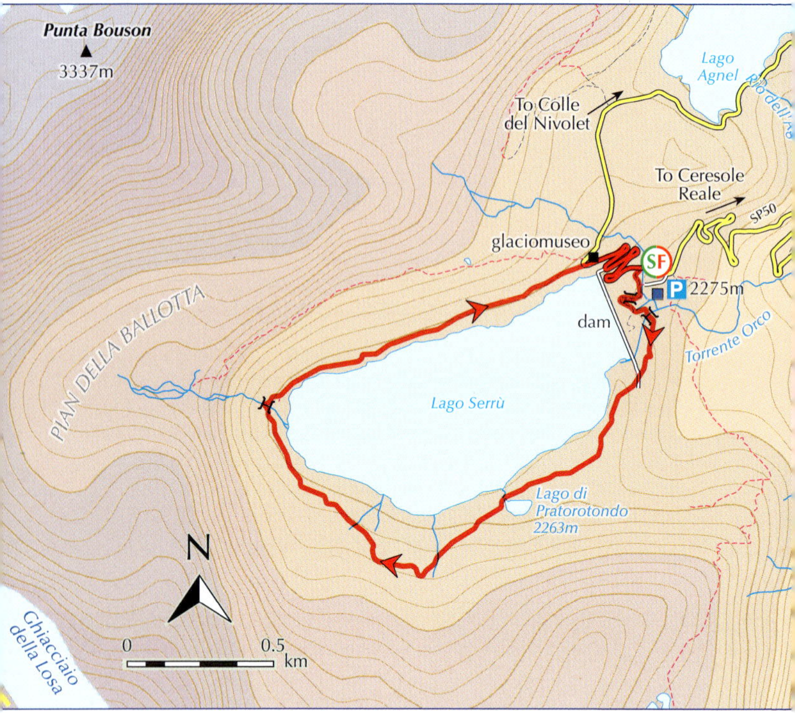

terrain. Modest tarn **Lago di Pratorotondo** (2263m) has transparent water in striking contrast to the milky turquoise of Lago Serrù.

Lago Serrù's water is cloudy with suspended rock dust and debris which causes the characteristic milky look, in sharp contrast to neighbouring Lago Agnel, crystal clear.

You climb over an outcrop, led on by upright stone markers and cross a bridge over meltwater streams in a marshy basin beneath immense moraine ridges and a glacier snout. Wind your way downhill towards the lake's westernmost end onto a path fashioned from slabs through fallen fractured boulders. A **bridge** leads over the impetuous cascading torrent of ice-melt from Pian della Ballotta, clouding the lake water.

A good 200 metres of **ice** used to fill this basin, exerting amazing pressure on anything below. As the weighty frozen mass moved at a snail's pace downhill, it dragged over underlying rocks, smoothing their surface, while stones and debris trapped beneath left recognisable grooves and scratches. The glaciers in this southernmost valley have retreated considerably over the last 100 years or so, and are currently losing at least a metre a year in thickness. They leave behind gigantic lateral ridges of fractured rock plucked off the mountainsides by the ice mass and transported valleywards.

Now you proceed above Lago Serrù's northern shore, a veritable botanical garden boasting hosts of orchids. This is an excellent angle for appreciating the Ghiacciaio della Capra opposite now; covered with a thick carpet of rock debris, it spreads down the lower flanks of Cima d'Oin. As you approach the road keep an eye out for the comical marmot colony that calls this home. Across the road is the **Glaciomuseo** (glacier museum) in a former electricity tower, a worthwhile visit.

With an eye out for passing traffic, walk down the road below the dam wall and back to the bus stop.

Looking back to the dam wall

WALK 22

Upper Valle Orco

Start	Chiapili Superiore
Finish	1882m bus stop
Time	5hr 15min (4hr 15min by exiting at Lago Agnel)
Distance	11.2km
Ascent	785m
Descent	660m
Grade	2
Access	Summer bus from Ceresole Reale en route to Colle del Nivolet stop at Chiapili Superiore on request.

This rewarding exploratory circuit sees relatively few walkers and all effort is amply repaid by glorious non-stop mountain views and vast alpine landscapes. A steady climb is followed by a delightful traverse on a good stretch of the old royal game track (see Walk 20 for a longer section). The descent is made on the wide zigzags of a remarkable old military track leading back down to the valley floor; dating back to the late 1930s it was intended as defence in view of the proximity of the border with France.

From the bus stop and scattering of houses that go by the name of Chiapili Superiore (1779m) walk down the road past grazing cows and a sculpted boulder commemorating the military origin of the road. At signposts fork L on n.539 aka Sentiero Videsott after the Park's early director, a committed environmentalist. Above the tree line, the path wastes no time in heading uphill E at first in tight zigzags touching on a string of ruined stone huts that once sheltered shepherds over the summer months. Views are vast and glorious from the word go, ranging to the lakes in upper Valle Orco as well as the Tre Levanne dominating the Ceresole Reale lake. You climb steadily in the company of a lovely cascading stream that encourages green alder shrubs while juniper and alpenrose prefer the drier slopes with colourful masses of wildflowers.

At **Alpe Muanda** (2370m) ignore n.538 and continue straight ahead, soon to cross a stream before veering W and becoming narrower and a little airy. At the signed **2497m junction** (2hr 30min) you join the renowned royal track. Branch

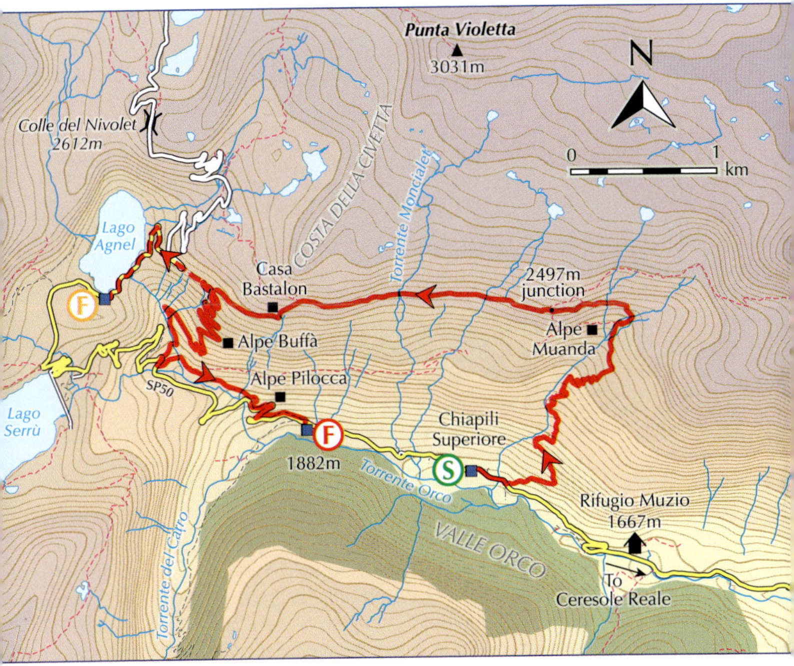

L on delightful n.550 which is soon wide and stone paved, touching on old barracks and cascading streams. Extensive glacially moulded rocks lie below but your attention will undoubtedly be concentrated on the awesome panorama up Valle Orco.

As the way starts to climb, some 30min from the 2497m junction, turn L on a clear but unmarked path in gentle descent to the nearby PNGP ranger's hut **Casa Bastalon** (2423m) set on a marvellous scenic outcrop.

A gentle path continues to a signed junction for n.537, the old military track (1hr 15min from the 2497m junction).

Exit to Lago Agnel bus stop (30min)

To leave the walk here keep straight ahead (WNW) to where the path ends at a bend in the road from Colle del Nivolet. Turn L in descent to the waterside of **Lago Agnel** (2297m) and along to the dam wall and the bus stop for the summer bus.

The Tre Levanne can be admired from the track

Main route

The main route n.537 aka Sentiero Chabod, turns L for the interminable long curves of the marvellously scenic lane, paved for the most part, it descends ever so gently. En route are ingenious mini-wells lined with stone to drain water off the road. After ruined **Alpe Buffà** (2234m) it finally drops to cross a bridge and head out to the road. A short tarmac stretch in descent and n.537 resumes L. This is Sentiero Bruno Tempo but after a second bridge you ignore the fork L and stick with the wide track SE. It's a saunter parallel to the road to **Alpe Pilocca** (1920m) a house with a flagpole on a corner. Follow the road to where the old track resumes L. Not far on as you approach a car park and bus stop (1882m, 1hr 30min) close to the opening of the Rio Carro valley, clamber down the grassy bank to the roadside.

Chiapili Superiore where the walk begins

Extension to Chiapili Superiore (1779m, 15min)

Continue on the old track for a further 10min then walk carefully down the road for 1km back to where you started.

WALK 23

Beneath the Tre Levanne

Start/Finish	Ceresole Reale (short variant: Villa)
Time	6hr 45min (short variant: 4hr 30min)
Distance	16km (short variant: 12.4km)
Ascent/Descent	1080m (short variant: 630m)
Grade	2–3 (short variant Grade 2)
Access	Ceresole Reale has year-round buses from Pont Canavese. In midsummer the bus to Villa at the northwestern end of the lake means a saving of 30min.

This rewarding itinerary in upper Valle Orco is dominated by the three Levanne peaks. The majestic pyramidal line-up forms a stretch of the Italian–French border. The walk as far as convivial Rifugio Jervis is straightforward and the ample panoramic flats and immense glacially smoothed rock slabs in the vicinity of the refuge are perfect for relaxing picnics. The continuation over Col di Nel is steep in parts; it sees fewer walkers but many chamois and marmots. Snow cover here can last into July. The complete walk circuit returns to Ceresole Reale, however an excellent short variant starts and concludes at Villa.

Signposts for Rifugio Jervis

Just up from the Bar Sport bus stop on the main road at Ceresole Reale (1620m), a stepped path for the *'Passeggiata Lago'* (lakeside promenade) turns down L. At the water's edge go R (NW) and soon past a windsurf launching spot, camping grounds, fields and the occasional house, and continue to the far end of the lake. Without forking L to Rifugio Mila, keep straight ahead along the road past a campsite and cluster of cafés of **Villa** (1583m, 30min). Immediately after a small chapel on the L is the start of path n.530 for Rifugio Jervis.

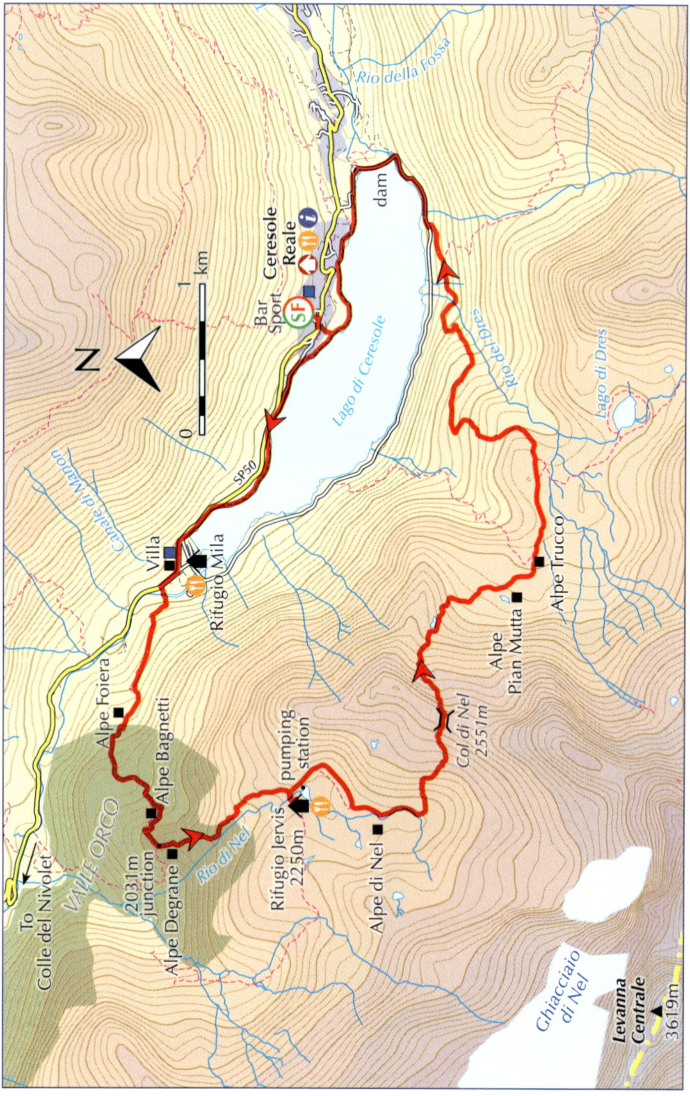

Rio della Fossa
dam
Ceresole Reale
Bar Sport
0
1 km
N
Lago di Ceresole
Rio del Dres
Lago di Dres
SP50
Canale di Manon
Villa
Rifugio Mila
Alpe Trucco
Alpe Pian Mutta
Alpe Foiera
Alpe Bagnetti
pumping station
Col di Nel 2551m
VALLE ORCO
Rio di Nel
Rifugio Jervis 2250m
Alpe di Nel
2031m junction
Alpe Degrane
To Colle del Nivolet
Ghiacciaio di Nel
Levanna Centrale
3619m

A clear path with occasional red paint splashes, it crosses a stream then begins its zigzagging climb W through a shady larch wood alive with song birds. **Alpe Foiera** (1823m) is the first of a series of old abandoned summer farms you'll touch on, beside a stream which is repeatedly crisscrossed. A second group of huts, **Alpe Bagnetti** (1882m), occupies a picturesque marshy area dotted with fluffy cotton grass and bordered by rowan trees. Larch and pink alpenrose shrubs then accompany you to a **2031m junction** (1hr 30min) and path n.531 from Chiapili di sotto.

Keeping straight ahead it's S now past the ruins of **Alpe Degrane** (2049m) and through a veritable sea of alpenrose shrubs. High above cascading Rio di Nel in its narrow gorge, the path winds upwards; at forks, take the *'consigliato'* (recommended) branches L. Up at glacially smoothed rock is a signposted fork at Pian di Nel (2256m). Keep R across a bridge and up to **Rifugio Jervis** (2250m, 45min). The well-run rifugio with helpful staff was named after a WW2 partisan and mountaineer from Ivrea, home to the CAI branch that owns the refuge. Its position is enthusing to say the least, before the three Levanne peaks which shelter the Ghiacciaio di Nel and its old moraine ridges. Furthermore it stands on the very edge of the panoramic Pian di Nel, an ample basin excavated by an extensive glacier and successively occupied by a milky lake, partly silted up.

Variant via Villa

For the short variant retrace your steps the same way you came to Villa and Ceresole Reale (2hr). But do not do so without taking time to explore this wonderful area first.

Main route

Back over the bridge fork R up below a chapel to the **pumping station** (connected to the Villa hydro-electric power plant) and follow n.526 skirting the easternmost edge of the basin. Keeping a watchful eye out for squelchy marshes head for the ruins of **Alpe di Nel** (2264m) and over a rise overlooking a veritable village of old stone huts. The way ambles its way essentially S. As you enter a final cirque, fork sharp L at a prominent cairn. Mostly SE-E the path climbs steadily and steeply over brightly flowered mixed rock-earth terrain, with some snow cover to be expected in early summer. Chamois are a common sight. **Col di Nel** (2551m, 1hr 15min) occupies an excellent position for appreciating the magnificent valley head. Silver-bearing lead was once mined in the vicinity. The clear descent path drops E over grassy flowered slopes via small platforms, helpful cairns showing the way. After a stretch alongside an old rockslip, you reach a boggy lake beneath the modest peak La Trucci. The path soon bears S dropping into a vast pasture basin. The flowers are brighter and thicker now, notably gentians and yellow

The Tre Levanne stand out above the Pian di Nel

avens. At what must have been a sizeable farming settlement (**Alpe Pian Mutta**, 2130m), pick your way through the ruins and across a shallow earth gully. Turn L along the grassy ridge to an old stone hut, **Alpe Trucco** (2098m, 1hr).

Ignore the fork R for Bivacco Leonesi and L downhill for Pouvens, and proceed E across marshy terrain, perfect for the tiny purplish-white flowers of insect-devourer common butterwort. A path turns uphill for Lago di Dres, but you descend NE (n.525/526) towards the large Ceresole lake. A broad lane on the water's edge is finally reached. Here turn R along to the **dam** wall (1582m) and cross it. Go L at the end over another wall then hug the lakeside around a point before forking R back up to Ceresole Reale (1620m, 1hr 45min).

WALK 24

Ceresole Reale lake circuit

Start/Finish	Bar Sport bus stop, Ceresole Reale
Time	2hr
Distance	7.6km
Ascent/Descent	130m
Grade	1
Access	Ceresole Reale has year-round buses from Pont Canavese. In midsummer the bus to Villa at the northwestern end of the lake means a saving of 30min.

The *giro del lago* (lake circuit) follows a delightful waterfront track and quiet surfaced road closed to motorised traffic save for a short stretch. All in all, it's a matter of gentle ups and downs. The lake is renowned for its cooling breezes in summer, much to the delight of windsurfers who appreciate the absence of motorised boats. The southern end is dammed while the northern end is home to a small hydroelectric power station partially built into the mountainside.

Ceresole Reale lake and the Tre Levanne

From the main Ceresole Reale (1620m) bus stop at Bar Sport near the Comune, walk towards the church. Just before Hotel Tre Levanne follow the steps L for *'passeggiata lago'* (lake stroll) down to the water's edge. At the bottom turn R on the wide track NW. Dominating SW across the lake are the magnificent pyramidal Tre Levanne peaks while at the far northern end of the lake are Punta Galisia and its neighbours, all of which mark the border with France. You wander along past a windsurf launch spot where there's usually some action, then come camping grounds, the occasional house and fields with grazing cows. In midsummer the way is lined

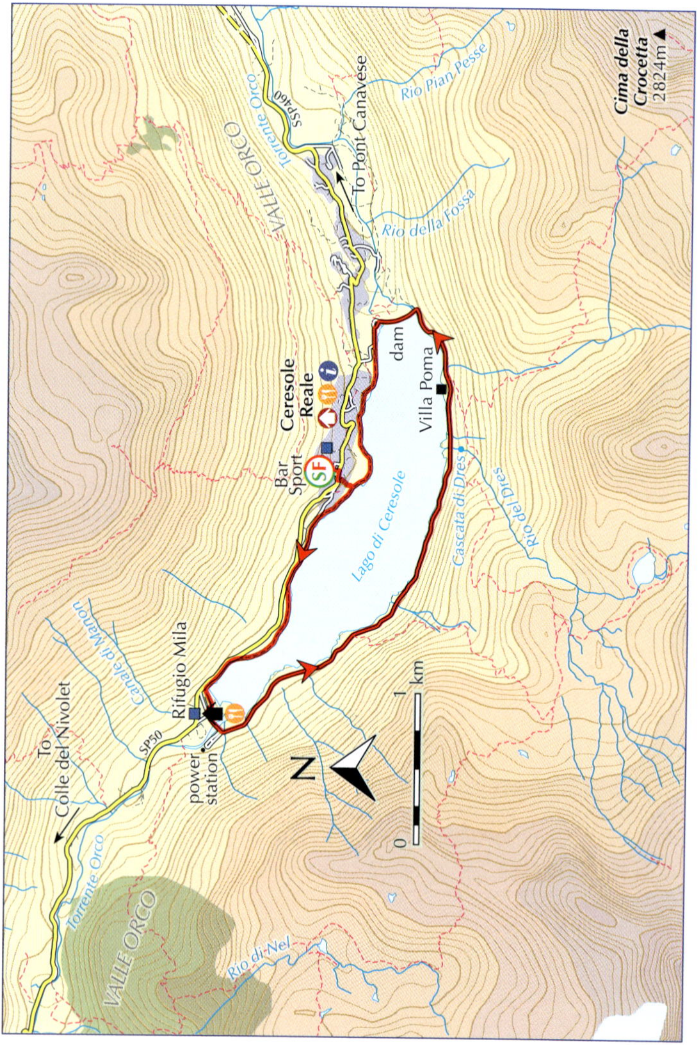
Cima della Crocetta
2824m
To Pont Canavese
Rio Pian Pesse
SS460
Torrente Orco
VALLE ORCO
Rio della Fossa
dam
Villa Poma
Ceresole Reale
Bar Sport
Lago di Ceresole
Cascata di Dres
Rio del Dres
Rifugio Mila
Canale di Manon
SP50
power station
To Colle del Nivolet
0
1 km
N
Torrente Orco
VALLE ORCO
Rio di Nel

The pleasant lakeside stroll after Ceresole Reale

with bright wildflowers from dog roses to scented pinks. At the lake end and a playground, turn L along the road past **Rifugio Mila** (1583m) and over a gushing stream past the modest power station and pylons. Stick with the tarmac along the shady wooded western shore for around 1km to where it's pedestrian only. Several old houses dot the way as do picnic tables beneath larch trees. Ignore paths turning uphill away from the water. It's a pleasant stroll with modest ups and downs.

The attractive crashing waterfall **Cascata di Dres** never fails to please. Continue on over old-style Villa Poma tucked in the trees on the lakefront. Not far on you branch L over the **dam** wall (1582m), offering a fascinating view up and down Valle Orco. At the far end is a 1931 plaque to the workers who lost their lives on the construction site. Go L onto a track over glacially smoothed rock slabs. Past more camping grounds and around a point you reach the signed stepped way leading back up to the bus stop at Ceresole Reale's Bar Sport.

WALK 25

The Old Villages of Valle Orco

Start/Finish	Bus stop at 1195m signpost for Sentiero Natura/Sentiero delle Frazioni Alte above Noasca
Time	3hr 30min
Distance	6.4km
Ascent/Descent	540m
Grade	1–2
Access	The walk start is approx 1.5km above Noasca via hairpin bends and is served by year-round buses that continue up to Ceresole Reale. Roadside parking is possible.

This peaceful round trip in Valle Orco along the 'Sentiero delle Frazioni Alte' (path of the high hamlets), follows an old paved way dotted with votive shrines threading through a string of medium-altitude villages from the 1700s, abandoned in the 1960s, mostly due to migration to the industrial cities for work. Communal buildings include chapels with colourful frescoes, a school and an oven for the traditional rye bread. After an initial climb, the way is mostly level, before a descent in lower Vallon del Roc leads back to the main road near the start point. Any time spring–autumn is suitable.

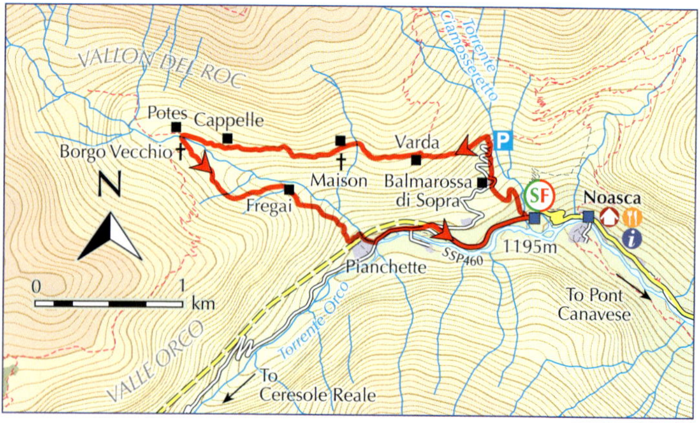

An old-style fridge known as a crutin

At the 1195m bus stop, look out for the national park wooden post for n.543 'Sentiero Natura' together with the 'Sentiero delle Frazioni Alte' and the red/white of the GTA (Grande Traversata delle Alpi). The path winds upwards through hazel trees to old terracing. A narrow asphalt road is joined through the hamlet of **Balmarossa di Sopra** (1275m). The old path soon reappears overgrown, climbing high on the bank of Torrente Ciamosseretto. After a couple more encounters with the road you reach a parking area (1356m). The path forks here – ignore the R branch which soon crosses the cascading torrent, and keep L on up past a shrine and onto a lane. This leads W for a short stretch before you branch R (n.543/GTA) winding uphill through woods of wild cherry, sycamore and chestnut and lined with dry-stone walls, niches fitted with shrines.

The first settlement, **Varda** (1500m), with its partially restored houses, is well worth an exploratory wander. Don't miss the crutin, back-breakingly low stone-roofed huts alias ingenious fridges – streams were diverted through them to cool dairy products.

The way continues W over streams and across terraces where sheep graze. Further around the hillside is **Maison** (1582m), the largest village. It boasts a whitewashed **church** decorated with paintings of saints. On the far edge of the settlement is the school complete with old wooden benches, chilly outside toilet and teachers' lodgings upstairs. It was in use until the mid-1960s.

The descent from Cappelle towards Vallon de Roc and its waterfall

A brief climb leads to a marvellous panoramic stretch on a cliff edge with giddy views to the Valle Orco road and underlying hamlets. Ahead W is the Cima di Courmaon. The next settlement, Mola (1591m), with its communal oven and frescoes, is the highest of this line of hamlets, followed shortly by **Cappelle** (1585m) which features a drinking fountain and fading frescoed saints. A short descent takes you to the cluster of huts of **Potes** (1500m) near a small dam and below a lovely waterfall in Vallon del Roc.

Across a bridge L, the path climbs onto a rocky spur below a **chapel** and the hamlet of **Borgo Vecchio** (1567m). At this point leave the red/white GTA to climb away to the R and and keep L as the Sentiero Natura begins its descent SE down the valley. Flowered pastures are crossed followed by a further brief climb. Once you have passed a side stream in light woodland, the path reappears in paved form intent on serious descent at last. Zigzags lead to the tightly-knit houses of **Fregai** (1428m). Now you drop unexpectedly into beautiful beech wood, which accompanies you the rest of the way to the settlement of **Pianchette** (1220m). Keep L following red arrows then R down to the main road. Turn L and proceed to where the road from Ceresole Reale emerges from a tunnel, in the vicinity of a bus stop (3hr 30min). Should you have parked at the start point, walk carefully down the road for 800m.

WALK 26

Rifugio Pontese and Lago di Teleccio

Start/Finish	Lago di Teleccio dam wall
Time	2hr 45min
Distance	7km
Ascent/Descent	450m
Grade	1–2
Access	From Rosone in Valle Orco drive up Vallone di Piantonetto on the narrow 10.5km road and park at the dam wall near the guardian's house. No buses come up here.

The route described here is a straightforward and very rewarding circuit with wonderful views. As the initial stretch as far as Rifugio Pontese is only faintly marked, it is inadvisable in low cloud or mist, whereas the return is wide and clear. A couple of days could profitably be spent at the friendly rifugio with side trips to neighbouring passes and valleys.

Rifugio Pontese (photo by Davide of Rif Pontese)

Start out from the car park at the wall of the Lago di Teleccio dam (1917m). Rifugio Pontese with its yellow shutters is visible N in a commanding position. Beyond it tower Torre del Gran San Pietro and massive Becco di Valsoera. Turn L and walk all the way along the 80m high, 515m-long **dam** wall and then go R (NW) to join a faint path marked with yellow paint splashes that heads across to the buildings of summer farm **Alpe Fumietto** (2152m). Continue N past long-abandoned **Alpe Mandonera** (2265m) and **Alpe Giafort** (2236m), and ignore a path forking L. Here you bear E to cross a bridge over Rio di Piantonetto and the junction with the path from Bivaco Carpano.

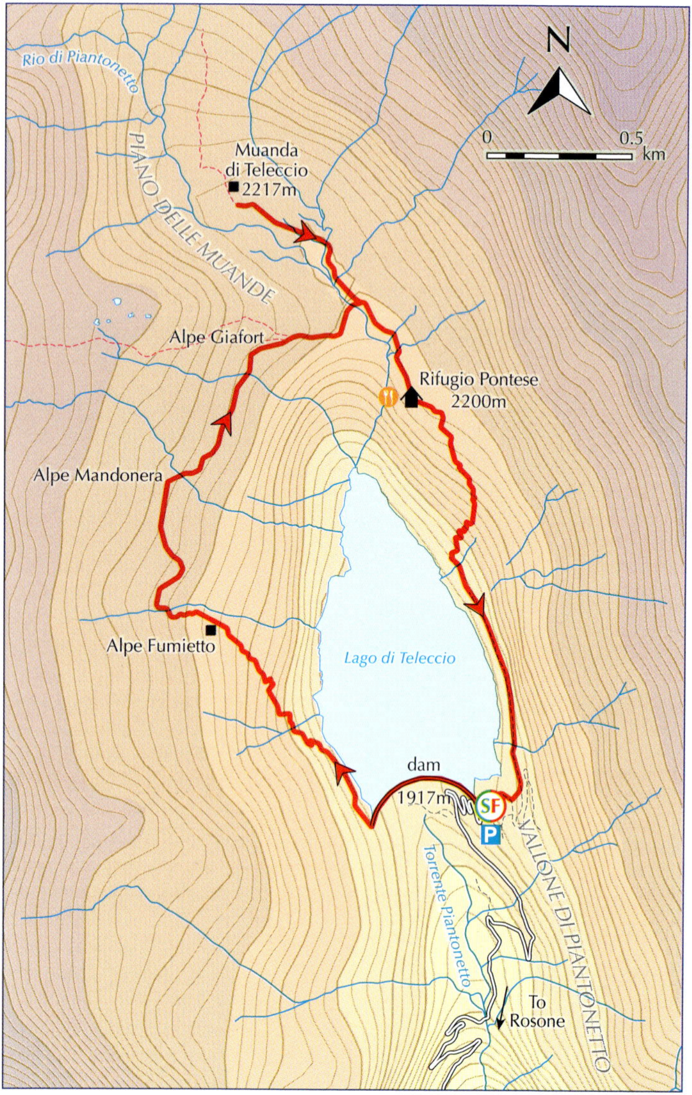
N
0
0.5
km
Rio di Piantonetto
PIANO DELLE MUANDE
Muanda
di Teleccio
2217m
Alpe Giafort
Rifugio Pontese
2200m
Alpe Mandonera
Alpe Fumietto
Lago di Teleccio
dam
1917m
SF
P
Torrente Piantonetto
VALLONE DI PIANTONETTO
To
Rosone

An ibex keeping an eye on Rifugio Pontese (photo by Davide of Rif Pontese)

Unless you prefer to head straight to Rifugio Pontese (and save 30min), go L on n.558 NW keeping to the R stream bank. It quickly reaches a glacial cirque and vast pasture basin watered by streams fed from the higher glaciers – Ghiacciaio di Teleccio (due N behind a rock barrier) and Ghiacciaio Roccia Viva (NW).

VALLONE DI PIANTONETTO

Lower Vallone di Piantonetto has towering gneiss flanks, which give an impression of desolation. The upper part was dammed for hydro-electricity in 1955, with the construction of a 23 million cubic metre dam on the site of a silted-up glacial lake. Above Lago di Teleccio is a beautiful ample grazing basin surrounded by vast rock shelves, precursors to a chain of imposing peaks the likes of Roccia Viva and Torre del Gran San Pietro. Sheltering in cirques are two surviving glacier pockets, which feed pasture and lake alike. A refuge stands on the edge of the basin, a testimony to the growing popularity of this wild and wonderful valley with walkers and rock climbers.

Lago di Teleccio (Walk 26) (photo by Davide of Rif Pontese)

The marshy terrain hosts specialised flowers such as the insectivorous common butterwort with its small purplish-white blooms, and the solitary whitish flowers of grass-of-Parnassus.

Not far along are the old huts known as **Muanda di Teleccio** (2217m), a high-altitude summer farm. According to medieval records, in 1206, the Bishop of Aosta granted the inhabitants of Cogne pasture rights here. Payment took the form of 30 cheeses to be delivered on St Martin's Day, 11 November. However, to reach the site the shepherds from Cogne were obliged to undertake a lengthy traverse – via 3304m Colle di Teleccio!

Today, in place of the livestock are large numbers of chamois and ibex – shy creatures who make for the surrounding slopes if disturbed. Marmots are not unusual either.

Retrace your steps to the junction then keep straight ahead, soon dropping to the vast glacially smoothed rock slab where homely **Rifugio Pontese** (2200m, 2hr) stands. An earlier hut built in 1889 when the surrounding peaks were being discovered by the pioneer alpinists, stood much further up the valley.

From Rifugio Pontese a clear path heads SSE in descent over a rock spur and winds down a rock flank (ignore the junction for n.560 to Rifugio Pocchiola-Meneghello). It widens into a broad track and follows the E shore of the lake to the jumble of derelict buildings and the Lago di Teleccio dam wall (1917m, 45min).

WALK 27

Nivolastro to Andorina

Start/Finish	Ronco Canavese
Time	3hr 30min
Distance	8.5km
Ascent/Descent	670m
Grade	2
Access	Ronco Canavese and Valprato are served by a year-round bus service from the railhead at Pont Canavese.

This beautiful and not-too-strenuous circuit explores two abandoned alpine hamlets set in marvellously scenic spots and rarely visited. It runs along the western flanks of Valle Soana, the name possibly derived from *suina*, pork-related, or alternatively *sana*, healthy, which the locals prefer. Thickly wooded, it has become popular with shy wild boar.

From the centre of Ronco Canavese (940m) not far uphill from the bus stop, take narrow Via Vittorio Emanuele uphill past the bakery to the old people's home (Istituto San Giuseppe) where you take a concrete ramp L, signed for Nivolastro.

Church at Nivolastro

After a stream crossing it becomes a delightful paved and stepped mule track climbing the steep mountain flank quite effortlessly in easy curves. Panoramic outcrop Mont del Trasi is followed by the first of a curious series of arched shrines dedicated to San Grato, the Madonna and others. The surroundings are beautiful woodland, both conifer and deciduous, inhabited by noisy nutcrackers. A curious monolithic stone watering trough precedes your arrival at the well-kept **church** of San Grato and drinking fountain at **Nivolastro** (1423m, 1hr 15min).

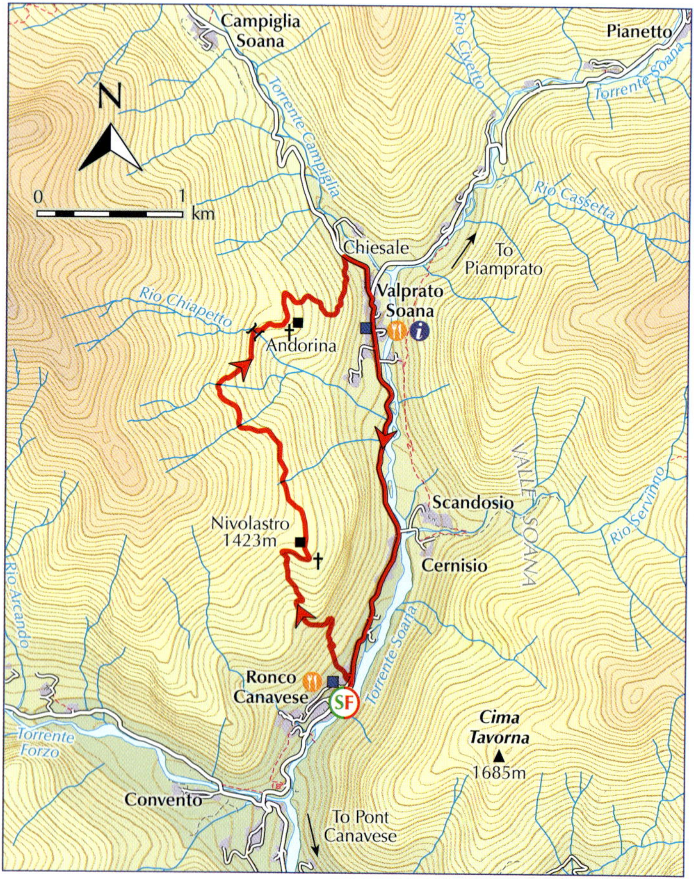

Ignore the signed path to Chiapetto and make your way past erstwhile elegant multi-storied houses with their iron balconies. With the exception of the ranger's premises, the hamlet is slowly and surely crumbling and giving in to ferocious creepers. And to think that over 20 families once called it home. On the far edge of the settlement take the narrow marked path N along old stone terracing walls and into woods, home to chamois. Larch and alpenrose grow side by side with huge ant hills. You find yourself climbing gently to 1521m to detour sheer rock outcrops. Cascading streams over glacially smoothed rock slabs are crossed on a **bridge**, then not far downhill is the scenically-set stone chapel and silent old houses of **Andorina** (1453m, 1hr).

After drinking in the wonderful views which take in the Rosa dei Banchi, set out on the path marked 'V' (for Valprato). It is a straightforward descent NE initially through pine woods then beautiful tall beech. You emerge on the roadside close to **Chiesale** and turn R for the short walk down to **Valprato Soana** (1116m, 45min) with its eateries and tourist office. Now either take the bus to return to Ronco Canavese or follow the road on foot (allow 30min).

WALK 28

Val di Forzo, Boschettiera and Bivacco Davito

Start/Finish	Tressi
Time	6hr (2hr 10min for Boschettiera)
Distance	11.6km (5.2km for Boschettiera)
Ascent/Descent	1100m (310m for Boschettiera)
Grade	2
Access	A car or taxi are essential for this walk as no buses run the 5km up to Tressi from the Bosco turn-off near Ronco Canavese in Val Soana.

Added to the Gran Paradiso National Park in 1979, quiet Val di Forzo branches NW off Valle Soana. Its northernmost fork culminates in a vast wild rock-strewn cirque in the shade of little-known giants Monveso di Forzo, Punta di Forzo and elegant Torre di Lavina. The walk follows an old paved path to the abandoned hamlet of Boschettiera, for a glimpse of long-gone medium-altitude alpine life.

En route are rock niches housing colourful frescoed votive shrines dating back to the 1700s, possibly the work of itinerant artists.

While the walk is very long, it's not difficult and the path is in good condition. Note: in low cloud or mist, common in these high valleys, orientation can be tricky above the tree line.

Just before Tressi (1185m), on the final curves of the road, marked path n.608 forks off L, bypassing the actual hamlet. Bearing L (N), it crosses a stream bed and proceeds between low stone walls through abandoned orchards and meadows. An easy climb through hazel trees brings you onto a rocky rise on the right bank of impetuous Torrente Forzo opposite old stone houses.

Steps cut out of the rock lead to a marvellous example of religious folk art, a wayside votive **shrine** under an impressive rock overhang. Dating back to 1748, it is often lovingly restored, hence the gorgeous colours of its multitudinous saints.

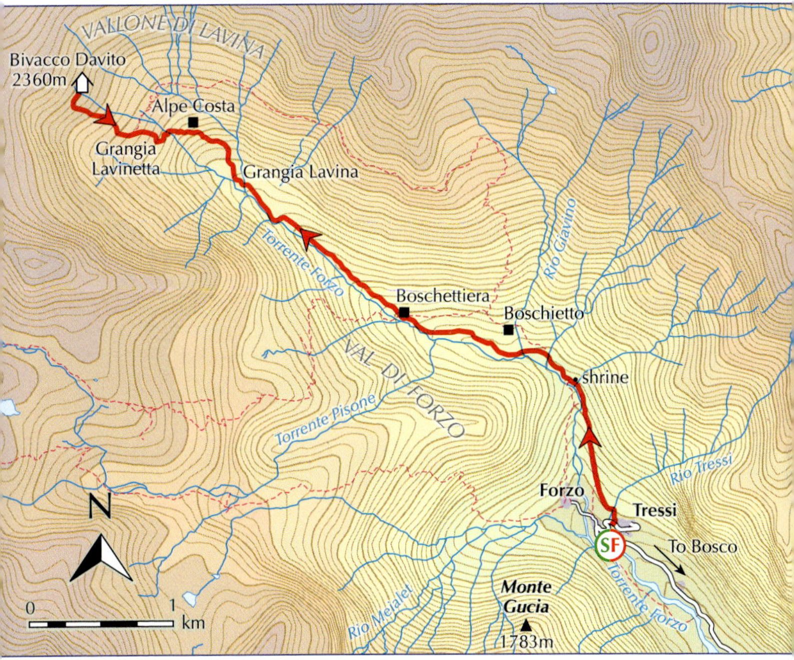

A side stream is crossed and the path continues climbing as the valley narrows. Next to a bridge ignore n.610 up R through swathes of yellow broom to the hamlet of Boschietto, visible on a rise with its white church tower (a worthwhile detour, time permitting). Stick with n.608 W alongside ice-blue Torrente Forzo through meadows with ash and sycamore trees to the once-thriving settlement of **Boschettiera** (1486m, 1hr 10min). Nowadays it has only a few summertime residents, drinking water and a communal oven, not to mention more frescoes.

This upper section of Val di Forzo is called Vallone di Lavina. Keep on up the R side of the stream, NW now. Steeper stretches pass through larch wood with plenty of wild berries. As the gradient levels amidst the last larch trees, the valley opens out with a lovely vision of a broad rock platform, legacy of an ancient glacier, beyond which is a light grey semicircular ridge. Torre di Lavina is N, and, despite its name, is more like a pyramid than a tower. You cross a small stream on boulders, then come to abandoned huts on a rise (**Grangia Lavina**, 1796m), with a second group huddling beneath a rock overhang a little further up. Consider

A frescoed shrine en route to Boschiettiera

yourself halfway at this point. The path bears L (W) to steps cut into the rock and a zigzag climb through alpenrose and green alder shrubs. In a pasture clearing studded with black vanilla orchids, a signboard reminds you these are the realms of the national park.

Yet another stream is crossed beneath a small waterfall, and you wind up to more old stone huts, **Alpe Costa** (1979m), where a rest will give you time to admire views SE down the valley. The grazing cows in the vicinity are brought up for the summer pastures. The landscape becomes more desolate with every step you take and the path is not always clear, although there are cairns and red paint splashes guide you. A further group of huts (**Grangia Lavinetta**, 2092m) stand in a lovely basin run through with rivulets which make for marshy terrain and wet feet. Curious low huts here with turf roofs are crutin, which, rather than providing dwellings for alpine dwarves, once served as cool storage of dairy products – precursors of the refrigerator.

Continue up past a collapsed hut, directly above which a sizeable cairn is visible (on the edge of the platform with the bivouac hut). The path, clearer now, heads L below it, with a final wide swing R to come out at yellow-painted **Bivacco Davito** (2360m, 2hr 30min).

> **Bivacco Davito** is a tiny basic metallic hut in an isolated position, making an overnight stay there a special experience. You'll need a sleeping bag and cooking gear, and water is available from the stream nearby.

Return to Tressi the same way, allowing 2hr 20min.

WALK 29

Sanctuary of San Besso

Start/Finish	Campiglia Soana
Time	5hr 30min (3hr 30min San Besso)
Distance	13.3km (7.3km return to San Besso)
Ascent/Descent	1050m (670m San Besso)
Grade	2
Access	The closest bus for Campiglia Soana is at Valprato Soana, 2.5km down the road.

This rewarding loop visits a photogenic sanctuary set on a rocky mountainside – a worthwhile excursion in its own right – before embarking on a beautiful panoramic traverse with the occasional crumbly exposed stretch. Marmots and a wealth of wildflowers are guaranteed, with chamois higher up. Relatively low altitudes are involved, meaning the walk as far as the sanctuary is usually feasible as early as May and as late as October, although this will depend on snow falls.

Campiglia has a shop and cafè-restaurant.

From the WWI cenotaph in the centre of Campiglia Soana (1350m), follow the road uphill NW past the car park. The way is soon closed to unauthorised traffic, and you turn R across a wooden bridge over Rio Campiglia. As the stream cascades away, you continue steadily upwards past a **shrine** and take the turn-off R for San Besso. Path n.625 climbs N through light woodland with elder and raspberry shrubs, while the open mountainside is thick with martagon lilies and purple orchids which attract colourful butterflies. A diagonal passage L climbs past a rock outcrop and up to an old hut (Grange Randonero, 1817m), with a good view NW to the upper valley.

The path veers left (N) to enter a side valley with simple summer farm, **Grangia Ciavanis** (1874m) not far from a lovely waterfall. The sanctuary buildings are visible now NE, in the shelter of the pointed rock overhang Monte Fautenio, on the lower reaches of Rosa dei Banchi. The way up the steep flank twists and turns, slippery underfoot at times due to the abundant greenstone. But you're rewarded by arrival at the **Santuario di San Besso** (2019m, 2hr) and the adjoining Ricovero Bausano bivouac hut. The meadows above the buildings are bright with purple alpine asters, pink thrift and felted edelweiss, perfect picnic companions.

Tête-de-la-Nouva
3034m
Pointe-de-Peradze
3021m
Punta dell'Asgelas
3021m
Rosa dei Banchi
3164m
Grangia Arietta
Colle Balma Arietta
2326m
Grangia Barmaion
Monte Diavolo
2308m
Alpe La Balma
Monte Fautenio
2072m
Santuario San Besso
2019m
Grangia Ciavanis
shrine
Campiglia Soana
Valprato Soana
PIANO DELL'AZARIA
VAL CAMPIGLIA
Rio del Rancio
Rio Arolei
Rio San Besso
Rio di San Besso della Balma
Rio Campiglia
Rio Fanton
Rio Civetto
Rio Balmassa
Rio Busiaire
Rio Giavino
Rio Chiapetto
SF
N
0
1
km

Felted edelweiss can be admired on the walk

The route continues on signposted path n.625 skirting beneath the church to head NW across flowered pasture. You cross several side streams, but keep to the R side of the main stream, Rio San Besso, for the time being. However, from the cluster of huts, **Alpe la Balma** (2152m), it's sharp L down across the stream bed. A clear path soon climbs a ridge W towards a depression. These southernmost flanks are carpeted with alpenrose, and chamois are often visible. At a saddle (**Colle Balma Arietta**, 2326m) don't be tempted by the cairns R (for Colle della Balma) but continue NW with Val di Campiglia opening up dizzily at your feet, and views W towards Torre di Lavina.

The narrow but clear way alternates ups and downs, with several stretches where the rubble-earth mixture has given way. The unstable nature of the terrain is due to the succession of different geological strata, and it can be slippery when wet, so take extra care. After contouring along the S flank of Rosa dei Banchi, you reach the old shepherds' huts of **Grangia Arietta** (2276m, 1hr 45min) in their pasture basin.

Ignore the path NW to 2939m Col d'Arietta, the connecting pass for Cogne. Go back briefly along the path you arrived on, then turn R on n.624. It drops to cross a stream near a waterfall. Larch trees provide meagre shade and the path winds down SSW, quite steeply at times. As the valley floor is approached, keep to the L of the farm buildings of **Grangia Barmaion** (1651m) to the vehicle access track. Once one of the king's game routes, it runs SE through the delightful Piano dell'Azaria, a quiet ample valley dotted with modest dairy farms. It's a pleasant stroll on the L bank of the river to the San Besso turn-off, and down to Campiglia Soana (1hr 45min).

SAN BESSO

An engrossing combination of ancient legend and Christian beliefs, centred on Besso, an early martyr and evangelist, comes into play here. A Roman soldier in the Thebean legion, in all likelihood dark-skinned, Besso escaped persecution in Martigny in 3rd century AD and took refuge in upper Valle Soana. However, after a period spent converting the local shepherds, he was hunted out and unceremoniously thrown off a high rock overhang. Not long afterwards, on 1 December (which then became the saint's day) shepherds located his body by digging where blood stains appeared on the snow.

Today a sanctuary in his name stands beneath that overhang, Monte Fautenio in Val Campiglia. Festivities are also held on 10 August, attended by processions of the faithful and hangers-on. Year in year out a group of pilgrims from Cogne cross a mountain pass to participate, consolidating age-old links. After the celebratory mass, the weighty statue of the saint, dressed as a Roman centurion, is carried around the sanctuary by bearers who vie with each other for the honour. A scarlet-robed priest leads the way bearing revered relics of the saint. In addition, fragments of greenstone are distributed as a lucky charm, as it is believed to have miraculous properties; San Besso was well known for his powers of healing.

The Santuario di San Besso beneath Monte Fautenio

WALK 30

Above Pramprato to Col Larissa

Start/Finish	Piamprato
Time	5hr
Distance	12.6km
Ascent/Descent	1050m
Grade	2
Access	A midsummer bus from Pont Canavese via Valprato Soana ventures up the ever-narrowing road to Piamprato.

On the easternmost edge of the Gran Paradiso National Park, this walk holds much of interest. Wide-ranging views are enjoyed from Col Larissa, a high pass linking with Chardonney in the Valle Aosta and long used by the locals. Likewise, the king's hunting parties used the 19th-century game track, lengthy paved stretches of which have survived, making it trouble-free for today's walkers. Wildflower enthusiasts will be delighted by the vast range, making midsummer the best time to go.

On the way to Col Larissa

From the car park and bus stop at Piamprato (1551m) head N straight through the village. Take the dirt road (n.630) NW alongside the stream Rio Piamprato to the farm buildings of **Alpe Prariond** (1643m) where the chair lift to the rifugio begins (it cuts 200m/30min off the ascent)

Purists will stick with the road climbing in wide bends between grassy banks touching on a 'big bench', to the buildings of eatery **Rifugio Ciavannassa** aka Rosa dei Banchi (1875m, 45min). Don't tarry here after dark as this was once the abode of a terrible witch and latecomers might encounter the bats from her retinue…

From here, the regularly marked path n.630 keeps high above the stream, ascending due N. You emerge onto a lovely flat basin brightened by pink

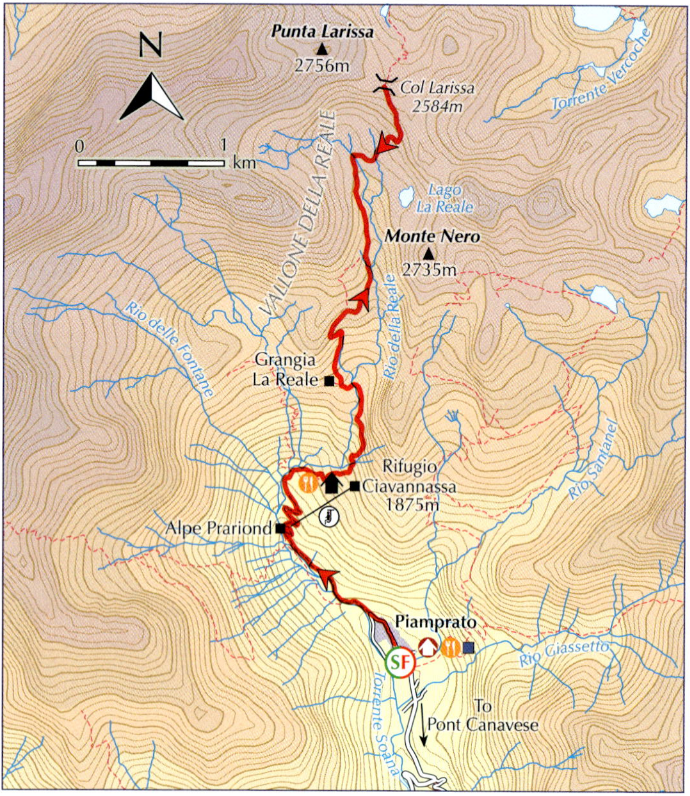

Lago La Reale and Monte Nero

alpenrose shrubs and cross the stream L, re-entering the domain of the national park. Not far up is old-style summer farm, **Grangia La Reale** (2095m) in Vallone della Reale. The King of Sardinia apparently had a lead mine in the vicinity which may explain the denomination 'royal'. On the other hand, it could derive from an ancient Piemontese word for 'stream'.

Primroses carpet the slopes as the path climbs easily through a series of upper valleys; the pass comes into view, easily identifiable thanks to a pylon.

To the NE is **Monte Nero**, another scene of evildoing. A devil once tricked the villagers of Piamprato into gathering below it to await the Madonna, who in fact appeared just in time to stop the rocks crashing onto the onlookers, as per the dreadful original plan!

At 2405m the path veers R across the stream. Cairns point you up to vestiges of the royal game track above picturesque Lago La Reale. You're led over grass studded with lilac round-leaved penny-cress, then rubble where glacier crowfoot blooms. A long diagonal stretch completes the ascent to the ample saddle **Col Larissa** (2584m, 2hr 15min), the name a derivative of 'larch'. In clear conditions the spectacular views range from the triangle of Rosa dei Banchi and its remnant glacier (WSW), then Monte Avic N towering over its lake, and hopefully the Matterhorn and Monte Rosa beyond. Views S even take in Monviso and the Maritime Alps.

Return to Piamprato the same way, allowing 2hr.

PIAMPRATO

As regards the village of Piamprato, few people winter over there now – the number currently stands at six, boosted in summer by holiday makers. The church and old stone buildings dating back to the 1700s point to a sizeable community in the past while the old school bears a 19th-century plaque expressing gratitude to the king, the benefactor. Nowadays it has a cafè-resto and accommodation, while further up the road is a chairlift (weekends only) as far as pleasant Rifugio Ciavanassa.

APPENDIX A

Italian–English Glossary

Italian	English
acqua (non) potabile	water (not) suitable for drinking
affittacamere	B&B
agibile (inagibile)	in good (bad) condition, referring to a hut or route
aiuto!	help!
albergo	hotel
alpage, alpe	summer pasture area and/or hut
alta via	long-distance high-level route
alto	high
altopiano, altipiano	high altitude plateau
autostazione	bus station
balma	old shepherds' dwellings with dry-stone walls
becca, cima, punta, testa	mountain peak, summit
bivacco	bivouac hut
bocca, bocchetta, col, colle, finestra, fenêtre, passo	mountain pass
borgata, frazione, hameau	hamlet

Italian	English
cabinovia, telecabina	gondola lift
caduta sassi	falling rocks
camere libere	rooms available
capanna, casolare, casotto	hut
capoluogo	provincial or regional capital or town
cascata	waterfall
casotto PNGP	park ranger's hut
cengia	ledge
comba, combe	long narrow valley
costa	flank, slope
cresta	crest, ridge
dessot/dessus	lower/upper
diga	dam
est/orientale	east/eastern
facile	easy
fiume	river
funivia	cable-car
ghiacciaio	glacier

Italian	English
grangia	stone shepherd's hut, used seasonally
lac (lacs), lago (laghi)	lake (lakes)
località	place, locality
locanda	guesthouse
mayen	medium-altitude farm that can be utilised early (such as May, hence the name) to provide livestock with fresh grass
montagna	high-altitude summer farm in Valle d'Aosta
muanda	high-altitude summer farm in Piemonte
navetta	shuttle bus
nord/ settentrionale	north/northern
ovest/ occidentale	west/western
palestra di roccia	rock-climbing area
passeggiata	promenade
pedonale	for pedestrians
percorso	route
pericolo/ pericoloso	danger/dangerous

Italian	English
piano	plain, plateau when a noun (cf slowly or quietly, when an adverb)
ponte	bridge
prato	meadow
Pro Loco	local tourist office
ricovero invernale	winter shelter adjoining a refuge
rifugio	manned mountain hut
rio, torrente	mountain stream
san, santo, santa	saint
seggiovia	chair lift
sentiero	path
soccorso alpino	mountain rescue
sorgente	spring (water)
stazione ferroviaria	railway station
sud/ meridionale	south/southern
tornante	hairpin bend
torre	tower
traforo	road tunnel
val, valle, vallon, vallone	valley

APPENDIX B

Useful contacts

Visitor centres of the Parco Nazionale del Gran Paradiso can be found at Ceresole Reale, Noasca and Ronco Canavese in the southern Piemonte section and Cogne, Chavaney and Dégioz in the northern Valle d'Aosta section. The fascinating Alpine Botanical Garden at Valnontey also doubles as an information point. See www.pngp.it

Useful tourist information offices, referred to as *Ufficio Turistico* or *Pro Loco*, are listed below. To call Italy from abroad use the country code +39 and include the '0' when dialling a landline. Numbers starting with '3' are mobiles.

Aosta
Tel 0165 236627
www.lovevda.it
This website covers all the villages on the Valle d'Aosta side of the Gran Paradiso park

Ceresole Reale
Tel 0124 953186
www.turismoceresolereale.it

Cogne
Tel 0165 74040
www.visitcogne.it

Dégioz
Tel 0165 905816

Noasca
Tel 0124 901001
https://proloconoasca8.wixsite.com/proloconoasca

Pont, Valsavarenche
Tel 0165 95304 (summer)

Rhêmes Notre Dame (Bruil)
Tel 0165 936114
www.rhemesturismo.it

Ronco Canavese
Tel 0124 817377 (summer)
www.vallesoana.it

Valprato Soana
Tel 0124 812908 (summer)
www.vallesoana.it

APPENDIX C

Rifugi

Rifugio Benevolo
Tel 0165 936143
https://rifugiobenevolo.com

Rifugio Chabod
Tel 0165 95574
www.rifugiochabod.com

Rifugio Ciavanassa
Tel 377 3983070

Rifugio Città di Chivasso
(Currently closed)
Tel 0165 905703
info@comune.valsavarenche.ao.it

Rifugio Grauson
Tel 0165 1756003
www.rifugiograuson.it

Rifugio Jervis
Tel 0124 953140
www.rifugioguglielmojervis.it

Rifugio delle Marmotte
Tel 389 3488785
www.rifugiodellemarmotte.it

Rifugio Mila
Tel 0124 953230
www.rifugiomassimomila.it

Rifugio Pontese
Tel 0124 800186
www.rifugiopontese.it

Rifugio Savoia
Tel 0165 94141
www.rifugiosavoia.com

Rifugio Tetras Lyra
Tel 380 1851926
www.rifugiotetraslyre.it

Rifugio Vittorio Emanuele II
Tel 0165 95920
www.rifugiovittorioemanuele.com

Rifugio Vittorio Sella
Tel 0165 74310
www.rifugiosella.com

DOWNLOAD THE GPX FILES

All the routes in this guide are available for download from:

www.cicerone.co.uk/1183/GPX

as standard format GPX files. You should be able to load them into most online GPX systems and mobile devices, whether GPS or smartphone. You may need to convert the file into your preferred format using a conversion programme such as gpsvisualizer.com or one of the many other such websites and programmes.

When you follow this link, you will be asked for your email address and where you purchased the guidebook, and have the option to subscribe to the Cicerone e-newsletter.

CICERONE

www.cicerone.co.uk

NOTES

NOTES

NOTES

NOTES

LISTING OF CICERONE GUIDES

BRITISH ISLES CHALLENGES, COLLECTIONS AND ACTIVITIES

Great Walks on the England Coast Path
Map and Compass
The Big Rounds
The Book of the Bivvy
The Book of the Bothy
The Mountains of England and Wales:
Vol 1 Wales
Vol 2 England
The National Trails
Walking the End to End Trail
Cycling Land's End to John o' Groats

SHORT WALKS SERIES

15 Short Walks Hadrian's Wall
15 Short Walks in the Lake District: Keswick, Borrowdale and Buttermere
15 Short Walks in the Lake District: Windermere Ambleside and Grasmere
15 Short Walks Lake District: Coniston and Langdale
15 Short Walks in Arnside and Silverdale
15 Short Walks in the Ribble Valley
15 Short Walks in Nidderdale
15 Short Walks in Northumberland: Wooler, Rothbury, Alnwick and the coast
15 Short Walks in the Yorkshire Dales: Grassington, Skipton, Malham and Ilkley
15 Short Walks in the Peak District: Bakewell and the White Peak
15 Short Walks on the Malvern Hills
15 Short Walks in Cornwall: Falmouth and the Lizard
15 Short Walks in Cornwall: Land's End and Penzance
15 Short Walks in the South Downs: Brighton, Eastbourne and Arundel
15 Short Walks in the Surrey Hills
15 Short Walks on Dartmoor North: Okehampton and Chagford
15 Short Walks on Dartmoor South: Ivybridge and Princetown
15 Short Walks on Exmoor
15 Short Walks Winchester
15 Short Walks in Bannau Brycheiniog: Brecon Beacons
15 Short Walks in Pembrokeshire: Tenby and the south
15 Short Walks in Dumfries and Galloway
15 Short Walks in the Trossachs: Callander and Aberfoyle
15 Short Walks on the Isle of Mull
15 Short Walks on the Orkney Islands
15 Short Walks on the Shetland Islands

SCOTLAND

Ben Nevis and Glen Coe
Cycling in the Hebrides
Cycling the North Coast 500
Great Mountain Days in Scotland
Mountain Biking in Southern and Central Scotland
Mountain Biking in West and North West Scotland
Not the West Highland Way: A Mountain High Way
Scotland
Scotland's Best Small Mountains
Scotland's Mountain Ridges
Scottish Wild Country Backpacking
Skye's Cuillin Ridge Traverse
The Borders Abbeys Way
The Great Glen Way
The Great Glen Way Map Booklet
The Hebridean Way
The Hebrides
The Isle of Mull
The Isle of Skye
The Skye Trail
The Southern Upland Way
The West Highland Way
The West Highland Way Map Booklet
Walking Ben Lawers, Rannoch and Atholl
Walking in the Cairngorms
Walking in the Pentland Hills
Walking in the Scottish Borders
Walking in the Southern Uplands
Walking in Torridon, Fisherfield, Fannichs and An Teallach
Walking Loch Lomond and the Trossachs
Walking on Arran
Walking on Harris and Lewis
Walking on Jura, Islay and Colonsay
Walking on Mull, Coll and Tiree
Walking on Rum and the Small Isles
Walking on the Orkney and Shetland Isles
Walking on Uist and Barra
Walking the Cape Wrath Trail
Walking the Corbetts
Vol 1 South of the Great Glen
Vol 2 North of the Great Glen
Walking the Fife Pilgrim Way
Walking the Galloway Hills
Walking the John o' Groats Trail
Walking the Munros
Vol 1 Southern, Central and Western Highlands
Vol 2 Northern Highlands and the Cairngorms
Winter Climbs in the Cairngorms
Winter Climbs: Ben Nevis and Glen Coe

NORTHERN ENGLAND ROUTES

Cycling the Reivers Route
Cycling the Way of the Roses
Hadrian's Cycleway
Hadrian's Wall Path
Hadrian's Wall Path Map Booklet
The Coast to Coast Cycle Route
The Coast to Coast Map Booklet
The Coast to Coast Walk
Walking the Dales Way
The Dales Way Map Booklet
Walking the Pennine Way
Pennine Way Map Booklet

LAKE DISTRICT

Bikepacking in the Lake District
Cycling in the Lake District
Great Mountain Days in the Lake District
Joss Naylor's Lakes, Meres and Waters of the Lake District
Lake District Winter Climbs
Lake District:
High Level and Fell Walks
Low Level and Lake Walks
Mountain Biking in the Lake District
Outdoor Adventures with Children — Lake District
Scrambles in the Lake District —
North
South
Trail and Fell Running in the Lake District
Walking The Cumbria Way
Walking the Lake District Fells —
Borrowdale
Buttermere
Coniston
Keswick
Langdale
Mardale and the Far East
Patterdale
Wasdale
Walking the Tour of the Lake District

NORTH-WEST ENGLAND AND THE ISLE OF MAN

Cycling the Pennine Bridleway
Isle of Man Coastal Path
The Lancashire Cycleway
The Lune Valley and Howgills
Walking in Cumbria's Eden Valley
Walking in Lancashire
Walking in the Forest of Bowland and Pendle
Walking on the Isle of Man
Walking on the West Pennine Moors
Walking the Ribble Way
Walks in Silverdale and Arnside

NORTH-EAST ENGLAND, YORKSHIRE DALES AND PENNINES

Cycling in the Yorkshire Dales
Great Mountain Days in the Pennines
Mountain Biking in the Yorkshire Dales
The Cleveland Way and the Yorkshire Wolds Way
The Cleveland Way Map Booklet
The North York Moors
Trail and Fell Running in the Yorkshire Dales
Walking in County Durham
Walking in Northumberland
Walking in the North Pennines
Walking in the Yorkshire Dales:
  North and East
  South and West
Walking St Cuthbert's Way
Walking St Oswald's Way and Northumberland Coast Path

DERBYSHIRE, PEAK DISTRICT AND MIDLANDS

Cycling in the Peak District
Dark Peak Walks
Scrambles in the Dark Peak
Walking in Derbyshire
Walking in the Peak District -
  White Peak East
  White Peak West

WALES AND WELSH BORDERS

Cycle Touring in Wales
Cycling Lon Las Cymru
Great Mountain Days in Snowdonia
Hillwalking in Shropshire
Mountain Walking in Snowdonia
Offa's Dyke Path
Offa's Dyke Map Booklet
Scrambles in Snowdonia
Snowdonia: 30 Low-level and Easy Walks — North, South
The Cambrian Way
The Pembrokeshire Coast Path
The Pembrokeshire Coast Path Map Booklet
The Snowdonia Way
The Wye Valley Walk
Walking Glyndwr's Way
Walking in Carmarthenshire
Walking in Pembrokeshire
Walking in the Brecon Beacons
Walking in the Wye Valley
Walking on Gower
Walking the Severn Way
Walking the Shropshire Way
Walking the Wales Coast Path

SOUTHERN ENGLAND

20 Classic Sportive Rides
  in South East England
  in South West England
Cycling in the Cotswolds
Mountain Biking on the North Downs
Mountain Biking on the South Downs
The North Downs Way
The North Downs Way Map Booklet
The South Downs Way
The South Downs Way Map Booklet
The Cotswold Way
The Cotswold Way Map Booklet
The Ridgeway National Trail
The Ridgeway Map Booklet
The Thames Path
The Thames Path Map Booklet
The Two Moors Way
Two Moors Way Map Booklet
Walking the South West Coast Path
South West Coast Path Map Booklet
  Vol 1: Minehead to St Ives
  Vol 2: St Ives to Plymouth
  Vol 2: St Ives to Plymouth
  Vol 3: Plymouth to Poole
Suffolk Coast and Heath Walks
The Kennet and Avon Canal
The Lea Valley Walk
The Peddars Way and Norfolk Coast Path
The Pilgrims' Way
Walking Hampshire's Test Way
Walking in Essex
Walking in Kent
Walking in London
Walking in Norfolk
Walking in the Chilterns
Walking in the Cotswolds
Walking in the Isles of Scilly
Walking in the New Forest
Walking in the North Wessex Downs
Walking on Dartmoor
Walking on Guernsey
Walking on Jersey
Walking on the Isle of Wight
Walking the Dartmoor Way
Walking the Jurassic Coast
Walking the Sarsen Way
Walks in the South Downs National Park

ALPS CROSS-BORDER ROUTES

100 Hut Walks in the Alps
Alpine Ski Mountaineering Vol 1 — Western Alps
The Karnischer Hohenweg
The Tour of the Bernina
Trail Running — Chamonix and the Mont Blanc region
Trekking Chamonix to Zermatt
Trekking in the Alps
Trekking in the Silvretta and Ratikon Alps
Trekking Munich to Venice
Trekking the Tour du Mont Blanc
Tour du Mont Blanc Map Booklet
Walking in the Alps

FRANCE, BELGIUM, AND LUXEMBOURG

Camino de Santiago — Via Podiensis
Chamonix Mountain Adventures
Cycling London to Paris
Cycling the Canal de la Garonne
Cycling the Canal du Midi
Mont Blanc Walks
Mountain Adventures in the Maurienne
Short Treks on Corsica
The GR5 Trail
The GR5 Trail —
  Vosges and Jura
  Benelux and Lorraine
The Moselle Cycle Route
Trekking in the Vanoise
Trekking the Cathar Way
Trekking the GR10
Trekking the GR20 Corsica
Trekking the Robert Louis Stevenson Trail
Via Ferratas of the French Alps
Walking in Provence — East
Walking in Provence — West
Walking in the Auvergne
Walking in the Brianconnais
Walking in the Dordogne
Walking in the Haute Savoie: North
Walking in the Haute Savoie: South
Walking on Corsica
Walking the Brittany Coast Path
Walking in the Ardennes

PYRENEES AND FRANCE/SPAIN CROSS-BORDER ROUTES

Shorter Treks in the Pyrenees
The Pyrenean Haute Route
The Pyrenees
Trekking the Cami dels Bons Homes
Trekking the GR11 Trail
Walks and Climbs in the Pyrenees

SPAIN AND PORTUGAL

Camino de Santiago: Camino Frances
Coastal Walks in Andalucia
Costa Blanca Mountain Adventures
Cycling the Camino de Santiago
Mountain Walking in Mallorca
Mountain Walking in Southern Catalunya
Spain's Sendero Historico: The GR1
The Andalucian Coast to Coast Walk
The Camino del Norte and Camino Primitivo
The Camino Ingles and Ruta do Mar
The Mountains Around Nerja
The Mountains of Ronda and Grazalema
The Sierras of Extremadura
Trekking in Mallorca
Trekking in the Canary Islands
Trekking the GR7 in Andalucia
Walking and Trekking in the Sierra Nevada
Walking in Andalucia
Walking in Catalunya —
  Barcelona
  Girona Pyrenees
Walking in the Picos de Europa
Walking La Via de la Plata and Camino Sanabres
Walking on Gran Canaria
Walking on La Gomera and El Hierro

Walking on La Palma
Walking on Lanzarote and Fuerteventura
Walking on Tenerife
Walking on the Costa Blanca
Walking the Camino dos Faros
Portugal's Rota Vicentina
The Camino Portugues
Walking in Portugal
Walking in the Algarve
Walking on Madeira
Walking on the Azores

SWITZERLAND

Switzerland's Jura Crest Trail
The Swiss Alps
Tour of the Jungfrau Region
Trekking the Swiss Via Alpina
Walking in Arolla and Zinal
Walking in the Bernese Oberland — Jungfrau region
Walking in the Engadine — Switzerland
Walking in Ticino
Walking in Zermatt and Saas-Fee

GERMANY

Hiking and Cycling in the Black Forest
The Danube Cycleway Vol 1
The Rhine Cycle Route
The Westweg
Walking in the Bavarian Alps

POLAND, SLOVAKIA, ROMANIA, HUNGARY AND BULGARIA

The Danube Cycleway Vol 2
The High Tatras
The Mountains of Romania

SCANDINAVIA, ICELAND AND GREENLAND

Hiking in Norway —
  North
  South
Trekking the Kungsleden
Trekking in Greenland — The Arctic Circle Trail
Walking and Trekking in Iceland

SLOVENIA, CROATIA, SERBIA, MONTENEGRO AND ALBANIA

Hiking Slovenia's Juliana Trail
Mountain Biking in Slovenia
The Islands of Croatia
The Julian Alps of Slovenia
The Mountains of Montenegro
The Peaks of the Balkans Trail
The Peaks of the Balkans Trail
The Slovene Mountain Trail
Walking in Slovenia: The Karavanke
Walks and Treks in Croatia

ITALY

Alta Via
  1 — Trekking in the Dolomites
  2 — Trekking in the Dolomites
Day Walks in the Dolomites
Italy's Grande Traversata delle Alpi
Italy's Sibillini National Park
Ski Touring and Snowshoeing in the Dolomites
The Way of St Francis: Via di Francesco
Trekking Gran Paradiso: Alta Via 2
Trekking in the Apennines
Trekking the Giants' Trail: Alta Via 1 through the Italian Pennine Alps
Via Ferratas of the Italian Dolomites:
  Vol 1
  Vol 2
Walking in Abruzzo
Walking in Italy's Cinque Terre
Walking in Italy's Stelvio National Park
Walking in Sicily
Walking in the Aosta Valley
Walking in the Dolomites
Walking in Tuscany
Walking in Umbria
Walking Lake Como and Maggiore
Walking Lake Garda and Iseo
Walking on the Amalfi Coast
Walking the Via Francigena Pilgrim Route
  Part 1
  Part 2
  Part 3
  Part 4
Walks and Treks in the Maritime Alps

IRELAND

The Wild Atlantic Way and Western Ireland
Walking the Kerry Way
Walking the Wicklow Way

EUROPEAN CYCLING

Cycling the Route des Grandes Alpes
Cycling the Ruta Via de la Plata
The Elbe Cycle Route
The River Loire Cycle Route
The River Rhone Cycle Route

INTERNATIONAL CHALLENGES, COLLECTIONS AND ACTIVITIES

Europe's High Points
Pocket First Aid and Wilderness Medicine

AUSTRIA

Innsbruck Mountain Adventures
Trekking Austria's Adlerweg
Trekking in Austria's Hohe Tauern
Trekking in Austria's Stubai Alps
Trekking in Austria's Zillertal Alps
Walking in Austria
Walking in the Salzkammergut: the Austrian Lake District

MEDITERRANEAN

The High Mountains of Crete
Trekking in Greece
Walking and Trekking in Zagori
Walking and Trekking on Corfu
Walking on the Greek Islands — the Cyclades
Walking in Cyprus
Walking on Malta

HIMALAYA

8000 metres
Everest: A Trekker's Guide
Trekking in the Karakoram

NORTH AMERICA

Hiking and Cycling the California Missions Trail
Hiking the Pacific Crest Trail
The John Muir Trail

SOUTH AMERICA

Aconcagua and the Southern Andes
Hiking and Biking Peru's Inca Trails
Trekking in Torres del Paine

AFRICA

Climbing Toubkal
Kilimanjaro
Walking in the Drakensberg
Walks and Scrambles in the Moroccan Anti-Atlas

NEW ZEALANDAND AND AUSTRALIA

Hiking the Overland Track

CHINA, JAPAN AND ASIA

Annapurna
Hiking and Trekking in the Japan Alps and Mount Fuji
Hiking in Hong Kong
Japan's Kumano Kodo Pilgrimage
Japan's Kumano Kodo Pilgrimage
Trekking in Bhutan
Trekking in Ladakh
Trekking in Tajikistan
Trekking in the Himalaya

TECHNIQUES

Fastpacking
The Mountain Hut Book

MINI GUIDES

Alpine Flowers
Navigation

MOUNTAIN LITERATURE

A Walk in the Clouds
Abode of the Gods
Fifty Years of Adventure
The Pennine Way — the Path, the People, the Journey
Unjustifiable Risk?

For full information on all our guides, books and eBooks, visit our website:
www.cicerone.co.uk